The Remarkable And Adventurous Capybara Tales

By Hess Moontasir

This book belongs
to
Cillian Quinn

46 Clearmont road
Teddington, England

Forward by Sophia Moontasir

This is a book written by my father, whose love of animals has been an inspiration, for constructing this fascinating and highly enjoyable story.

The plot has many exciting twists and turns, yet the outcome will still surprise you.

In addition, the amazingly adventurous animals, will encounter challenges that shall provide you with wonderful excitement and immense intrigue.

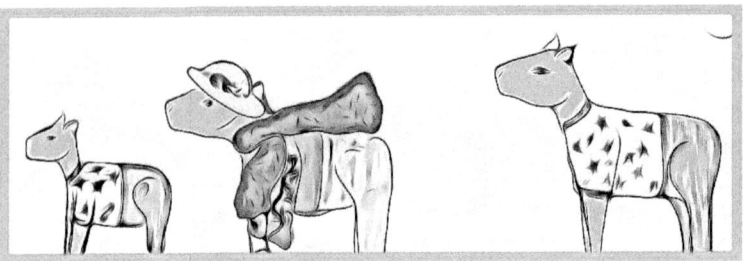

Acknowledgements

This book is dedicated to my family, my wonderful wife Gulia and two amazing children, Alen and Sophia. Also, it is dedicated to all animal lovers and to young readers.

The front cover design idea was undertaken magnificently by Sophia. Also, she made splendid story suggestions.

A big thank you to my superb family. Keep on living great adventures of your own.

Please kindly note, this story (and the images) were registered with the UK Copyright Service on the 29th July 2022 (Registration number 284742383).

Copyright © 2022 Hess Moontasir. All rights reserved.

Contents

Chapter 1 - The Awakening 5
Chapter 2 - The Unusually Unusual Arrival 20
Chapter 3 – Alas, Together Again 40
Chapter 4 - Rolanda-Runa Absorbs the Dream 49
Chapter 5 – The Island: A Loving Reminisce 61
Chapter 6 - The Dream's Transmission and Revelation 85
Chapter 7 – The Dream's Analysis 101
Chapter 8 - The Library Search 117
Chapter 9 – Entrance to the Other World 137
Chapter 10 – An Encounter to Remember 153
Chapter 11 – The Room of Hatches 169
Chapter 12 – A Resurgent and Rekindled Friendship 177
Chapter 13 – Kerisay Senior Reunited 193
Chapter 14 – SSK1 Returns 201
Chapter 15 – Soliloquy 212
Chapter 16 – Rolanda-Runa's Farewell 217
Appendix – A to Z of Rolanda-Runa's Spells 222

Chapter 1 - The Awakening

The normally wonderful and ebullient, yet tranquil female capybara looked pensively around at what appeared to be the darkened and desolate surroundings.

A sudden, severely savage, once in a "century" and torrentially brutal storm was merciless. The capybara gazed around with mouth agape, supplemented with a degree of considerable and naturally unusual nervousness, plus with a heightened sense of trepidation — at what remained of a now distinctly unfamiliar ambience, on the Island World of the Capybaras.

A special individual, known as Rolanda-Runa (in a past life formerly called Runena-Sabrieahiya) was a genially gentle capybara, possessing dulcet tones. In addition, to being truth be told: one of a kind, quite phlegmatic, as cool as a cucumber in almost all situations that required nous and immaculately attired (for a capybara).

She was loved by all of the island's inhabitants, due in no small measure, to her innate warmth, pious consideration of the needs of others, humility, and generosity.

Likewise, she was respected and praised for her indefatigability, which quite frankly reinforced her determination to further succeed.

What's more and without a doubt, she was helped by having inherited skills from an antecedent wizard.

Rolanda-Runa always wore a nylon necklace, with twenty-one small, perfectly spherical and intricately coloured stone beads, each colour triplet representing a hue of the rainbow.

Whenever she walked on her two hind legs, the beads glowed warmly.

However, she tended to conceal the necklace under her pink blouse and red coloured scarf. The necklace was only revealed to her husband and son, on two previous occasions and that was by accident, which she promised to herself would never be repeated.

Despite everything, when asked about the necklace's properties, she would claim that she had no idea why it glowed and how it worked.

Moreover, she would never explain when she had received it and would vaguely say it was her mother's dying wish that she inherited the necklace.

Her mother did ask her to foreswear to not speak to any animal about the power of the necklace. Only a very special and uniquely talented capybara would be permitted to wear it.

Remarkably, the power the necklace could harness was utterly mind-blowing according to Rolanda-Runa's mother, but it had to be used with the utmost care.

Yet Rolanda-Runa could relay a positively loving spell on those within her immediate family, who would believe they were praying to their gods of the capybara world.

Anyway, on this 25th of April day, in the year 2163, this harsh and devilish storm had heavily pounded and rocked Rolanda-Runa's pretty island home, to the very foundations of its core. This storm was unlike any that had ever been seen before or in any capybara living memory. In addition, its remorseless, and merciless nightmare had unleashed an appallingly wanton wave of traumatizing destruction.

It prompted many older residents vociferously to reflect on how they never could have imagined (even as they fled in every compass direction), the ferocity of the storm.

Rumbustiously, intense and wild winds of up to one hundred and twenty-two and a half miles per hour had incessantly hammered the coastline, completely shattering ancient and proud trees, as well as uprooting homes in the process.

Horrifically, bridges were swept disdainfully away, as if they were inconsequential or just little old and used toys that had passed their sell-by date.

But there was a chill in the air... a distinctively unwelcome chill. A peculiarly strange and fraught atmosphere echoed everywhere, in every nook and cranny.

Now, from the devastation that had torn and brutally gnawed away at the coastal area of the island, beneath the dangerous cliff's edge, to the north-west of the nearby capybara town, an energy locked within a hitherto secret hidden cave was stirring.

The identity of this energy form would later be explained to all and sundry on the island, but at this juncture in the story, its revelation of course, would be principal to nature's elements.

Anyhow, through the ages, the cave, in its very distant past, had been used by the skilful and secretive relative of Rolanda-Runa. Her ancestor, a wise wizard, was so skilled in his varied crafts that it was told, he could lock away uncompromisingly mean and spitefully negative energy forces.

These forces were colloquially and ubiquitously known in ancient times as the Mad-Bad-Dream-Fixers (MBDFs).

In point of fact, a very long capybara time ago (nearly one hundred years, give or take a few), the cave had been hermetically sealed and a spell was placed upon its entrance to protect the island from this cruel energy form, which would cause daily storms of untold misery.

Alas, it appeared something was incrementally moving in the inner sanctum, considerable depths (scores of metres) away from the cave's entrance.

Legend has it, that this inner sanctum, would magically lead automatically into an even deeper series of caverns.

Nonetheless, stealthy, slow slurping sounds could now be heard resonating pitifully from the depths of one contained chamber, enough to pull one's heartstrings, because it sounded too vulnerable and distressingly sorrowful.

But this was a dastardly deception!

The single ball of energy inhabitant had been dramatically awoken from its eternal sleep.

The horrendous and merciless storm had caused the enveloping trees to thunderously crash down on the ravishing island, plus the meticulously cultivated landscape and its terrain endured a viciously, violent vibration that had cracked the seal of the energy's jail and simultaneously woken the dark and menacing entity from within the depths of the wicked and foreboding cave.

Indeed, this electric energy form, fearfully termed the Siren-Spirit-King-One (or just SSK1), was also known to the capybara wizard from yore.

Somehow, SSK1 was the only survivor of this malignant group of spirits that had been imprisoned together. Having absorbed its compatriots, SSK1 was now a ball of malevolent energy.

Incidentally, the SSK1 deliberately and wilfully omitted the nomenclature, for its fellow and pitiful energy forms, as they were being consumed one by one.

Ultimately hard-fought for peace, had been bequeathed to the capybara descendants, following decades of conflict. To the inhabitants of this world, their home was a potentially idyllic paradise of an island and that was due to the heroic wizard. In fact, snatching victory from the jaws of the originally impending defeat of the energy forms, had come at a terrible cost, as the formidable wizard, it was told had tragically perished in a final and all-consuming battle an eon ago.

Consequently, the miscreant C-Echelons (a bizarre short form for the Elite-Capybaras) in a power vacuum, rose inextricably and mechanically to the zenith.

The pompous C-Echelons used ceremonial stilts to raise their height by thirty centimetres to demonstrate that in their mystical belief, those whom stood on two hind legs would be the most trusted.

Notwithstanding, there is always a quid pro quo in such matters. Since the end of the conflict, when almost a century had elapsed, a subsequent and sustained period of tranquility and relatively harmonious peace had ensued and it coincided with weather that was wonderfully clement all year round, except for the occasional and manageable rainstorm and sly surveillance orchestrated by the C-Echelons.

But for a capybara, a century was inordinately long, forever even.

The craft of wizardry had naturally been declining and fading into a distant memory.

Unquestionably, the teaching of magic and the interest in harnessing the powers of nature's elements, whom ancient capybaras had referred to as their gods, had somehow faded — slowly and inexorably slipping into oblivion.

There were the occasional rumbling rumours too, which trickled down towards the C-Echelons, who feared even an inkling of the distant mention of magic could undermine their superiority (rebellious ones viewed this as an iron-like grip), meaning discontent had the potential to ignite quickly like wildfire.

Ergo, the C-Echelons felt they had no alternative, but to deliberately influence "chitter-chatter" through the ultimate pain of deportation to one of the other islands.

The C-Echelons had throughout almost 4 generations (each in their world was twenty-five years) gradually attained hereditary power and influence; they wanted to remain dominant and wealthy. Nepotism was at its core.

Hence, this dominance was passed down to close relatives, as well as obedient and loyal friends.

Furthermore, all matters regarding home constructions or extensions, events, meetings, refuges, prescription of medicine, and education had to be approved by the C-Echelons, who would first require obsequiousness of varying degrees: worship or a large food payment in advance, if the request was particularly significant.

Likewise, the C-Echelons were not in your face oppressive per se. Fifty percent of the time they gave their agreement without any qualms and on other occasions a nod and a wink would suffice.

But they conveyed a sense of being "benign" dictators — particularly concerning significantly specific matters or repeated requests, alluded to above.

Do not forget that their less so endearing qualities reared its ugly head regarding any mention of the bygone wizardry practices.

Even so, they showered benevolence of a sort when they needed to — at sporting or annual events, when they had to be noticed during the awards ceremony.

Their approach was from their perspective of having "benevolent" control, and on balance, even if one played ball, everything else on the island could hardly be described as "laissez-faire".

When new regulations were being considered for taxing purposes, there would be the usual collective and rhetorically trite statement from the leadership of the C-Echelons.

"What would be at all wrong with just another tax imposition on families to help us, as your rulers to organise matters?" would be pontificated.

That epitomised how out of touch the C-Echelons were with their indescribably shallow money-grabbing statement. Perhaps their hubris was partly informed by the absence of daily magic, which meant the powers would crucially wane They like all the other animals, would have been cogent with the dire consequences, for openly practicing magic.

Thus, to all extent and purposes, as far as most of the island's inhabitants were concerned, the originally immense wizardry powers had consequently been abandoned and for them — had disappeared into the ether.

Coincidentally, in these seemingly (relatively speaking) modern capybara times, it was absolutely and deliberately frowned upon to suggest that a capybara could possess a special gift.

"The old ways were the bad ways and the older generations were not modern," would be the pointed cry and mantra of the younger and bubblier, partygoing capybaras.

No doubt, this perception had been influenced by the C-Echelons, who would twist the partygoers' arms to demonstrate loyalty and pressurise them to spy on their friends and families.

Returning to the clear and present danger, though previously, in a weakened and parlous state, the SSK1 had gradually and mercilessly managed to absorb all other energy forms that had been trapped with it, within the darkened chamber prison and was just trying slowly but surely, to now, literally bide its time and wait to pounce at the right moment!

SSK1 indelibly knew how to sustain itself and began immediately to incrementally weave dastardly plans for survival.

It was as if the light of the world had turned instantly to darkness, a bright and glowing candle had been extinguished, all at the flick of a surreptitiously sneaky switch.

Incontrovertibly, even the most minuscule thread of light could stir SSK1 into action. This is what sadly occurred. Also, to prosper on land, it could exploit the intense heat of the island's blazing astronomical Sun, whose rays of light were in temporary abeyance, due to the severity of the storm.

Moreover, the not-so irrational and isolated energy form still had the wherewithal to influence storms using cunning 'tricks' up its proverbial sleeve.

Crucially, its sorcery required above all else, to absorb a considerable amount of abundantly joyful energy from the capybaras on the island, who thrived contentedly.

This hungry energy acquirement applied to a lesser degree, even to the small, conceited cabal of C-Echelons.

The fruit the capybaras ate produced a happy and bouncy feeling and the SSK1 could not stand the capybaras feeling positive at all. The negative energy form was a thorough killjoy!

The underhand SSK1 planned to swap its "indescribably dull", negative energy with any "captured" capybara's positively gleeful ones. The capture would even mean a dream acquisition of the captured capybara's descendant.

Plus, the instant energy swap would instil a palpably negative and tiresomely repetitive dream into the victim's mind, which would then have its creatively felicitous capybara energy gradually absorbed by SSK1, whereby the vanquished animal would begin feeling tired and palpably listless forevermore — finally disappearing.

Alternatively, SSK1 could fiendishly and viciously inflict enduring sadness on its prey and the victim would be prone to the cruel energy's blackmail, plotting, scheming and spying.

Only a capybara with the gift could ever dream to have the wherewithal of tackling or repelling a bad dream and ultimately repel a foe like the SSK1 and deter its soaking up the ebullient characteristics of a capybara.

Nevertheless, this particular and effervescent female capybara, Rolanda-Runa, was on her way home from an exciting and lengthy weekend shopping expedition and unfortunately on this most fateful of occasions, dolefully on her own.

Earlier in the day and contrastingly, she had also been enthusiastically illustrating her charitable qualities, by buying nutritious food for the poorer and frailer capybaras.

This purchasing was greatly facilitated by using the island's currency called the Woody-Dragon-Eye, which was a highly sought-after luscious and sweet fruit that could be bartered for abundant crates of other types of appetising island fruit.

Yet it was worth noting, that the island's idyllic tranquility was abruptly shattered by the suddenness of the blistering storm's arrival, causing Rolanda-Runa and all of the capybara's island inhabitants in the north-west region considerable alarm; a great number of the capybaras were understandably perturbed and completely disorientated.

"Safety has to be sought first and foremost!" was the cry from the capybaras.

Soon, many older capybaras realized the inherent danger and took their first option and instinctively fled from the epicentre of the storm, with an injection of unforeseen energy (as in recent times many tended to party or be quite lackadaisical over the weekends) and in a sign of understandable panic, hurriedly scootered to the safety amongst the majestic hills.

Other more mobile ones careered down, in the direction of the magically formed underground earth bunkers, whereupon they tried to find any hiding place (initially even in the long grass adjacent to marshes, rivers, and ponds before better judgement subsequently made them think otherwise).

Whilst the rest huddled in a large colourful herd within their respective collections of the beautiful Java kapok trees that were incidentally, also established alluringly around the entire island in regions, at forty-five-degree diagonal compass point locations with reference to the centre of the island. These trees were the protectors.

Reassuringly, the regal Java kapok trees, positively enchanted, were also positioned in protective circles and within strategic localities.

They had this innate structure from time immemorial. Their branches would act as powerful and resilient, stern shields against any foe, storm, or other existential threat.

Whilst there was this innate sense of fearful behaviour being exhibited by the capybaras; relatively far away in the gloomy and foreboding cave, a more resonant and evil sound was being evoked, bouncing off the walls. It was defiantly strong and more omnipotent than seemed possible.

An echoing screech was followed by an interminable wailing cry, which shook the nearby surroundings, as if the energy form was trying to repudiate its home and lambast it for perceived treachery.

Unmistakably, the sound emanating from the bowels of the cave was now nauseating to anyone who heard these terrifying sounds or was within earshot.

The SSK1 was gaining power and signalling a barbaric intent that was nothing less, than one layered with malign ferocity.

It was moulding and fermenting trouble with its sorcery.

Chapter 2 - The Unusually Unusual Arrival

The dark, deadly and uncompromising energy form was now very much alive. It was alert! No longer dormant, but able to sow awful and pitifully, piteous plans. Its insatiable desire for energy was unremitting and it sought greater power.

Slowly, but surely, there was a harnessing of all of its being into one finite collection. Moreover, it was energetically attracted to this planet's massive Sun, like an impressive magnet, gathering a formidable force.

It saw the chink of light from its contained chamber and began sneakily, atom by atom, escaping. It was patently patient.

Focusing its "maturing", mighty mind, the energy form sensed and remembered the energy sources on land that could be harvested. To that end and to achieve its nefarious aims, it realised that it must first disable the protectors of the capybaras.

Its sorcery began dispatching signals to determine what area should be combated initially. Its mendacious plan was set.

First, the north-west would be subdued, then the conquering of the south-west, followed by the demolishing of the south-east and then the vanquishing of the north-east region. The acquiring of all the regions would mean complete dominance and the opportunity to possess unlimited power, as well as control time and space.

Incidentally, the north-west was certainly the prize of all the regions, in terms of the social fabric of the society and its harmony. These capybaras were mainly open and friendly, plus out of all the regions they tended to pray the most. Furthermore, there were just a very few capybaras residing there, who though, admittedly could not control magic, they still had the potential to communicate telepathically.

The C-Echelons appeared to have complete dominance over all the regions, except in the north-west, which was most interesting. From the perspective of the north-west, the other regions had a penchant, for being a little unruly and not complying with directives, which kept the C-Echelons busy. The distance between the regions helped keep potential territorial conflict at bay too. Regardless, the only common regional link would be the C-Echelons, who were loathed.

SSK1 learned quickly from its long hiatus and recognised that the Java kapok trees intrinsically sheltered the indigenous capybaras. This was just the beginning!

The SSK1's actions were an insidious forewarning of what was to become. Mentally jostling and jousting, like a sword fighter with the first north-west battalion of Java kapok trees (whereby each battalion had its alpha), as if first teasing them, then testing their resolve, SSK1 demonstrated an unmitigated desire for supremacy. The trees reacted and shook violently, whenever the dreadful energy issued threatening messages.

Then, SSK1 thrashed and swaggered, with an excruciating THUD, SPLAT, BAM, CRACK, followed by the delivery of an extraordinary cascading, BOOM, BOOM, BOOM!

SSK1 was now completely free!

Solemn silence pervaded the capybara world for a few precious, watershed moments. At this juncture, the island's inhabitants (particularly the C-Echelons) would have been forgiven for wishing, if the ancestral and wizarding powers had been respected and not dismissively overlooked (abandoned some claimed).

SSK1 continued and persisted. It persevered. It then focused.

First, second upon second, then minute upon minute, its unremitting control of the storm festered, bending the element to its will, generating a resonating sensation — shaking the capybara world. Then, SSK1 feeling more dominant, directed the pummelling of the surroundings, by the torrential and tormenting wind to continue. Battering, booming, crashing, slamming, and whooshing, all in an ear-splitting, unstopping, crescendo of bewildering sound.

Penultimately, above the ground and moving with secretiveness, SSK1 forged ever more powerful and mental strong-arm tactics, and the "cerebral" arm twisting mechanisms pervaded and the tussling showed signs of success.

It snapped off the peripheral, exhausted sapling Java kapok tree branches, as if these valiant guards were a trifling nuisance, an inconsequence. Finally, a prolonged striking of the trees persisted, for them to submit and surrender.

Indeed, SSK1 was able to stupendously convince the senseless, out-of-control storm to believe the trees were its ancestral foes.

The apparently indomitable storm was trying to be not just punitively bothersome, but demonstrating an unashamedly cruel streak, in its pursuit to demolish the trees, and tarnish the landscape forever.

This, in turn and without exception damaged all potential capybara events, which included the island's highly valued north-west hosting of the annual weekend fruit shopping bonanza, when the most luxurious range of fruit was on offer throughout the region, for an amazing half-price or less.

Matters got even further out of hand. SSK1 began to turn its attention to the uprooting of the less robust and outer ringed Java kapok trees in order to isolate the wisest and most graceful of all the old Java kapok trees, called the North-West Alpha (NWA). Particularly beautiful, but heavy looking, this specific NWA was a goliath of a specimen in this world: absolutely towering at 150 feet in height and with a trunk in excess of 9 feet. It was strategically located in the middle of a circular arboreta, in the north-west of the island.

Thus, the NWA being surrounded by its brethren, had a first line of defence — protecting the ensconced capybara homes and charming shops.

Then again, how long could the brethren hold out?

The capybara homes located nearer the outer-ring were indiscriminately and ruthlessly targeted and in the apparent, uncompromising midst of the storm's possessed mindset, its strong winds now deliberately and wantonly attempted to be far more than a typical aberration from a usual run-of-the-mill storm.

Indeed, what now ensued, would have caused abject consternation to all the C-Echelons, as the storm trashed through one corner of the weakest defence line; tearing branches off the trees (perfectly at 45-degree angles) that were protecting the homes.

The branches proceeded to fly off unerringly, like deadly spears and pierced the food shops of the capybaras with spiteful intent.

Anyway, the other and more resolute outer-ringed Java kapok trees had myopically believed their defence was unbreakable, now alarmingly witnessed how some capybaras fled to the centre, huddling fearfully together near the NWA, which actually, was a historical safe respite for these gentle creatures, if they felt threatened.

But then the panic-stricken animals, fearing utter destruction, began scurrying away further behind the NWA, towards all the other possible or perceived exits, horrified that their tree protectors would be soon roundly defeated.

In the intervening period, within a secret corner of the outer ring of trees, concealed among the debris, the hidden Rolanda-Runa was alone and slightly disorientated. She had been completely unprepared from the onslaught.

Rolanda-Runa, was still, more than one hundred metres away from the perceived safety of the wonderful NWA and in her current confused shaken state, momentarily oblivious to the ancient wizard's magically secret passageway to her own north-western island home, via the massive trunk of the NWA.

Earlier, the defenceless capybara, who though unnerved still had the wherewithal to ease rhythmically, elegantly and swerved majestically around the falling branches and hide.

Yet, the entranced storm sensed Rolanda-Runa's isolation (not her precise location) and enraged snapped off large branches from nearby and heavily weakened Java kapok defenders. Comparing the prized branches, two were chosen.

These distinctive outer-ringed trees miserably protested to the storm and swayed their grey branches in fear and not as a warning to rebuff and deter any further advancement.

The entranced and cruel storm shrieked in excitement, which alarmed Rolanda-Runa and without cover, revealed the vicinity of her vulnerable position. She was the prey!

Sensing harmful progress, the storm supplemented venom, spitting out immeasurable thunder and lightning to force the trees into a hasty retreat — arching backwards like feeble catapults, in a sign of abject submission.

Thereupon, the cunning and barbaric storm took delight in witnessing its fiendishness and took aim with the branches.

Imparting an additional negative mind control on them, SSK1 ordered the branches to advance, like demonic fighter pilots, whereupon the branches sought out their hapless victim and flew a little further on, like a menacing drone about to strike.

The identification of Rolanda-Runa's specific whereabouts was being honed in on.

Wishing to permanently disrupt and impede this capybara's kindly intentions of helping others (through inducing monumental fear), the hijacked branches fashioned a semi-circular motion and deceptively so, swung around and in a horizontal position, with great alacrity, it thunderously pierced the ground around her legs and the tremendous aftershock (for a capybara that is) caused the already unsteady female to sway unsteadily on the back of her legs, causing her to fall, roll over and lose her shopping.

The world around her was spinning.

At that moment, she became thoroughly lightheaded and collapsed in a heap — concussed.

Her magical necklace crashed to the ground and seemingly scattered into tiny and irretrievable fragments (from the enemy's perspective).

Forlorn Rolanda-Runa, looked on in abject desperation. The necklace was a prized possession.

On top of that, her fine-looking paper shopping crossbody bags were torn asunder and its contents comprising of succulent fruit looked now entirely inedible, bludgeoned and much worse for wear than could ever have been imagined: squashed from all sides and its delicate skin exposed from the ferociously battering winds.

The punitively possessed storm energised itself and its formed countenance laughed mendaciously at how the food was ruined, whereupon it moved "contentedly" on, to crush other opponents and sow the seeds of irreversible fear.

Time excruciatingly passed by slowly, it seemed to crawl... and SSK1 used this space to reflect upon its horrible achievements and savour in its unsavoury and unpalatable desires to cause sadness and merrily looked at the aftermath, of the vanquished land.

In the meantime, the female capybara at first struggled to move and then eventually staggered to her feet, but her surroundings looked rather unnervingly unfamiliar.

Slowly, she tried to think of her beloved family. That tended to bring her a sense of focus and keep her feet on the ground, so to speak.

Her head began to gradually clear, prompting her to instinctively ponder about her magical necklace, which could still help, but the potency of the attack had forcefully removed it from her.

Reeling around, she managed to see remnants of her necklace and with a small tear of joy in her eyes, she soulfully and meticulously picked up what she could find.

To others, panic would have been etched on one's mind, heart and soul, but she could more ably in the past, harness emotions with greater ease, when her powers had apparently been limitless.

"Where was my husband and son? Were they safe? Had they fled like the others or had they hidden in the basement of the home?" she gasped rapidly, whilst trying earnestly to control her feelings.

It was her husband's ingenuity in constructing the basement, principally because he was an expert in house building and this type of design in the world of capybaras was so innovative – much to the chagrin of the despised C-Echelons, who had disavowed this innovative development idea. Any favourable idea was challenged by the C-Echelons.

One small painful step followed another; she staggered on. She gradually began to identify the known landmarks and became inch by inch more reassured. Inspirationally, she tried to think passionately, positively and briefly reminisced about her magnificent mother, who had only recently and tragically passed away. Truly, her mother had been the only surviving member from the special wizard family, whose power for a time was unrivalled.

In contrast, Rolanda-Runa's husband never liked to talk much about his family or his parents, though he did explain how he had been placed in a care home and brought up by a religious order of capybaras, who were disciplinarians. Relevantly, residential and care homes were located in the south-east of the island. These care homes had been ruthlessly taken over by the C-Echelons in perpetuity, for financial gain.

There was much to admire about the capybara world, if one kept a low profile, did not rock the boat of the leadership, or veer adventurously beyond the respective regional domain.

To complicate matters, Rolanda-Runa and her family, as well as other capybaras, were also fearfully wary about the dwellers from one of the adjacent islands and how they might take advantage of the current precarious situation.

Nothing was spoken out aloud about the other three outer islands. Only one in particular, with a bearing of 315 degrees from the north-west regional home of Rolanda-Runa, was viewed with utter and unspeakable horror.

That scary place was home to shockingly bad tempered, strangely cumbersome, translucent green coloured and venomous predators, called the Furious-Bygone-Snakehead (FBS) creatures, which had multiple (eight in fact) shape-shifting heads and moved like sneaky, surreptitious, sly, slimy snakes.

Their enormous, three-foot-wide heads could modify their shape, but they would constantly wear these rather nonsensical and completely ridiculous righteous smiles, which were unedifying.

The incongruous necks of the FBS tended to be rather long and spindly. When excited, they would get tangled up with the other necks, which appeared terribly amusing.

By the same token, these creatures were not impressive communicators!

Their discussions could end up fairly confusing and lead to recklessly heated arguments. When they were annoyed, they could alter their appearance at the drop of a hat and pretend to be like any other type of FBS monster.

Beyond the known exterior islands, nothing new was learned by the younger generation, and the silent stories — only their eyes spoke — that once had been enthusiastically passed down from one generation to the next had all, but disappeared.

Now, these tales had either been terminated abruptly, for no clearly stated reason; helped no doubt by the C-Echelon induced changing work patterns, coercive threats, plus a perceived and slow disappearance of the ancient wizard generation.

As a result, both old and young, tended to avoid discussions about the world beyond their adored island, as the dangers were too scary to consider.

The Vast-Great Sea (VGS) and the strategically outlying islands (all most definitely unsettling), were thoroughly off-limit topics of conversation, and understandably so.

Three of these "other" islands were covered in a deep, silent eeriness and inhabited by the darker than the darkest clouds imaginable, making visibility nigh on impossible.

If any questions were inadvertently raised about these particularly fearsome looking clouds, or the world beyond the VGS, it was frightfully told (without always clear evidence) that silence from the oldest and appointed regional capybaras (agents of the C-Echelons), would be demonstrably ushered in and become prevalent and immediately demanded.

Anyhow, debris from the mighty trees had impacted the landscape and a significant number of the delightful capybara buildings had been sadly and distressingly crushed.

The wicked winds had channelled debris around and created an artificial, temporary, in certain places a somewhat fragile sea bridge crossing from the mainland to the FGS island.

Undeniably, the bridge points were not universally safe, yet the landmark was still palpably crossable, if so desired.

Attitude, was largely dependent on the mood of the translucent green and temperamental creatures and whether or not they had rested sufficiently. They could move with alacrity and finesse if they were motivated enough by hunger.

Rolanda-Runa intrinsically perceived danger in the air and that her family and friends could be in existential danger. More so, if the fearsome creatures escaped.

Fortunately, on this fortuitous of occasions, the green creatures had been distracted by the savage storms pounding the north-west region and uncertain of whether crossing the bridge, would be worthwhile or profitable for them, as they collectively sensed that the island's inhabitants would be in hiding and not out in the open for easy pickings.

In any case, Rolanda-Runa would always, her immediate family believed, pray to her gods to ask for divine intervention, when there was danger. In her distinctly unique world, prayers and poems were a euphemism for magical spells. She was not sure how the wind would blow when it came to the FBS, so time was of the essence.

The silence coalesced her thinking process, to address her vulnerable situation.

Rolanda-Runa bowed her gracious head and closed her pretty eyes in silent and resolute prayer.

With her magic necklace no more, her focused cogitation thus extraordinarily revealed, from out of nowhere, isolated beads from the remnants of the necklace, amongst the grass and leaves. She gingerly reached down and grabbed the three compliant red beads from the shaken earth beneath her feet.

Pulling a piece of thread from her pink blouse (the scarf had been lost), she quickly and ingeniously fashioned a bracelet, which was placed delicately above her right foot.

It was through sheer luck that she had managed to rescue the red beads, as they represented the first colour of the rainbow and its strongest wavelength. It would provide her with the power to end the storm, carry her to safety and to shield her with a protective light.

Momentarily, the distant roar of the despicable green FBS creatures could be heard and consequently she closed her eyes more tightly, mercifully unaware that the monsters had abstained from any invasion on this occasion, because there was no clear consensus for an invasion, amongst them.

Embattled, this particular capybara had a special gift, but she was neither in the brightest of moods nor feeling strong, after earlier losing her consciousness.

But she was determined and passionately gripped a single red coloured bead and uttered the following, which was a poem that came to her naturally, a sort of sixth sense.

Divine goodness that pervades our island world,
Shine the godly light, transmit and unfurl.
Protect capybara island from any harm.
Stop the storm in its tracks and bring us calm.

Protect the north-west region,
Let us harness strength and be a legion,
To deter any fiendish foe that tries to crush,
Reject, push away, demarche and flush!

Protect my family, protect my son,
Return me home, be at peace, to have won.
So, my family can thus reunite,
I plead for hope, salvation, a breather, and respite.

Some issues surround us,
But in our hearts, we have an inner brightness.
Give me strength and a sense of purpose,
Not be punished or locked within a foe's deadly circus.

This poem comes naturally to me,
How and why, can't say, but I want to be simply free.
So godly light, protect I plead,
End our torment and do this with speed!

Now, bring me respite, to be not alone.
Take me home!
With haste and speed,
Family reunite — I humbly ask for you to accede.

As she gritted her teeth, and repeatedly concentrated with even greater fervour, entreating its implementation, remarkable changes began taking place.

The storm clouds in the north-west region, surprisingly began to gradually first be placed in abeyance.

Then it miraculously retreated, without even a whimper and the angry tidal waves began to fall dramatically silent, at an instance.

One could have heard a pin drop, for a few treasured moments. The storm — seemingly pacified, immobilised, and sanitised.

She could also agonisingly feel one of the stone fragments from a red bead, mostly dissipate into a powder like material.

Grasping tightly, she held on to the last few miniscule pieces in sheer hope, then in anything else.

Unexpectedly, even the bridge crossing appeared to melt away too at a magical stroke and as a consequence, the sensing SSK1 was dumbfounded.

"What had defied me? How dare this take place! I am the only FORCE! It is destined... to be a unipolar world."

It was then succeeded by a pitiful moan, "What if the other regions: the south-west, south-east, and north-east could show this resistance and defy my ultimate goal of dominance?"

The hypothesis that resonated in the deep recess of the twisted mind of SSK1, albeit on this occasion at least, was that he had met an unexpected match and he promptly retreated... to reflect on the next evil move.

Rolanda-Runa began to feel giddy once more and then lost her consciousness.

With a blurred vision, utterly drained, she veraciously collapsed.

Extraordinarily, her inherited wizardry powers had been invoked by the spell and that innate clairvoyance generated an incredible and enchanted shadow, which serenely raised her frame and tenderly transported her, through the magical NWA passageway, to safety, whereupon she was gently placed, not far from the vicinity of her beloved home.

Time stood still, as the glow around Rolanda-Runa began to undulate. It was a sign that she was badly weakened.

With every ounce of courageous fibre left, she repeated the divine prayer and something magically occurred next.

A spellbinding and loving cradle light now gently elevated Rolanda-Runa's body and soon coaxed her slow advance in the direction of her cherished home, spinning floating beams of joyous light to demonstrate its beautifully protective core.

The delicate light appeared to hold Rolanda-Runa in its arms at specific times, when she began to wobble and then assist her with her movement forward.

A serene veil of loving positive energy surrounded her and seemed to glow radiantly, as she approached the extensive grounds adjoining her delightful home. It was surreal. A protective and heavenly shield was watching her every move.

Chapter 3 – Alas, Together Again

"Mother, mother, wake up! It is Kerisay your son," tearfully demanded the young capybara, in an imploringly controlled tone.

In moments of joy, sadness or fear, certain capybaras from the north-west region, had been known in the past, to break out in a poetic "prayer". Through a friendly contact, a so-called "remedial" transfer of knowledge would be sensationally generated and passed automatically between the individuals, if there was a direct bloodline, a marriage bond or a very deep friendship.

Though in a parlous state, Rolanda-Runa had still managed to send her message and her son had retrieved a source of magical inspiration, without even knowing.

It was tricky, for the mother to undertake this process successfully, as her son's mind (like his father's) was not always open and unusually extreme, or conflicting emotions could hinder or corrupt transfer implementation.

Unwittingly, Kerisay though desperate for his mother's revival, surprisingly considered a quatrain poem with an ABCB rhyme scheme. His mind on this occasion was mercifully more alert than usual and using a wonderfully rich vocabulary and a sense of rhyme, Kerisay elucidated the following with compassion and unexpectedly with complete composure.

Mother, finally you are home,
A relief, alive, miraculously true.
With open arms, welcome back and
Remember our brave searching hearts didn't eschew.

To cling on to, there was sadly no news.
Neither small nor big. Neither old nor new.
No shade and difficult circumstances prevailed,
This, we sadly did purview.

We were under a malicious, merciless
And ferocious attack that did not subdue.
We tried in vain, but change… occurred,
Strangely, belatedly… on cue.

Finally, tempest clouds lifted,
Life resurrected, to break an illegal curfew.
Shall celebrate your return and plan,
With, no trifling impromptu.

Now your home and safe to prosper,
Awake dear mother and listen to my voice
And be strong once more.
Share our expectations and rejoice.

Immediately, at having recited his poem, he proceeded to scooter and hop around his mother (in what appeared to be a sign of blind panic), while she remained silent, still and yet, somehow looking wonderfully elegant.

This tendency to run around in panic was also, not uncommon for young capybaras, but in the case of Kerisay, he could not see his mother moving, which prompted his reaction. A triggering of stress occurred and anxiety levels started to fluctuate wildly.

Seeing the condition of his son, the father spoke reassuringly, "Be patient my son and wait. Pray and be composed."

The son ran over to his father, who embraced his son. The loving warmth emitted by the father's embrace, precipitated a sense of calm discipline into the environment. Almost at once, they began to develop a pensiveness in controlled silence, with closed eyes. Their unified minds, vividly remembered the events that had transpired only a very short time ago. It was their flashback.

Earlier and serendipitously so in the circumstances, this reflectiveness had given them a growing understanding of their recent past. At the time, barricaded in the home basement, they were alerted to anomalous activity outside their isolated home and were drawn to this, like bees to honey.

Their minds recollected how she had been slowly floating, then extraordinarily appeared to walk on her two hind legs, the final short distance towards their village home, completely soaked, dishevelled, and somewhat rather disorientated, from their perspective, as she was not speaking and her face was emotionless.

Memories flooded back explaining why they could not leave their abode, due to the ferocity of the storm. Every time, they tried to open their ash grey coloured front door, it was slammed shut in their faces, with a menacing growl and startling vengeance, in a sign to warn them of the consequences, if they were to venture outside. They sensed that venture would be in pain of death.

The father and son recalled that they had no choice, but to bide their time, remain strong, and pray more fervently, for a miracle and an intercession by their gods. That miracle fortuitously had borne fruit, through the following prayer they had uttered in rapport.

Gods from all the ages,
Help and protect us.
Let Rolanda-Runa be safe,
With no negatives, just a plus.
Give us strength, calmness,
Patience, to elicit no fuss.
As we earnestly pray,
Reunite us, without delay.

Retrospectively, having kept a constant lookout through the front door spy hole for Rolanda-Runa (the father and son occasionally rotating their sentry observations), their prayer had given them an added sense of purpose. In the main, the alert father was checking for his wife, whilst the son had decided against taking a lengthy refuge in the basement, due to his understandable nervousness, at the unfolding events.

Finally seeing his wife on the other side, via the spy hole in the front door, had completely changed the husband's facial countenance and brought a smile of relief to his face (and his son's when he had been called from the basement).

Coincidentally this momentous reuniting of the family, had also seen a rather sudden and dramatic quietening of the weather, as if an unknown negative force had simply given up the fight and resoundingly enunciated, "Enough is enough!"

The change in the ambience outside immeasurably lifted the heart of the father Kerisay Senior. It had brought a spring in his step. By the way, his real name was Kerisay-Kerisaya, as many capybaras on the island had the Kerisaya in their names. Rolanda-Runa preferred calling him Kerisay Senior, as he tended, in her eyes, to behave at times with a sense of unnecessary seniority, when he spoke to his son, which Rolanda-Runa chastised him for. But the name Kerisay Senior stuck and as she was the controlling influence in the home, Kerisay Senior just went with the flow.

The anamnesis continued. The father and son speedily removed the remaining front door barricade vestiges and rushed out of their home; whereupon they tenderly managed to safely guide Rolanda-Runa, ever so gently inside the house. Within the resplendent living room area, she collapsed, as the magical cradle light had disappeared; its job was done!

As the father and son were closing the front door together, they recognised that the storm had strikingly evaporated, but the remnants of the devastation had been left everywhere and were eye-wateringly tragic. Kerisay and his father looked at each other and felt utterly helpless and for that moment, bereft of hopeful energy.

With apparently none of the more austere, sacerdotal, and older capybaras around; they had fled or were hiding. Hence, the father and son could not ask or seek any medical advice. They were simply praying for divine intervention.

As their eyes finally opened, releasing the evocation, they could feel that seconds had turned into inordinately long minutes and minutes into tortuous hours.

The interminable wait began to precipitate feverish worry, yet suddenly and quite miraculously Rolanda-Runa stirred and then gently commenced breathing, but it was noticeably irregular, which was naturally troublesome.

Kerisay Senior responded and placed his face gently next to his wife's and prayed quietly and silently. It was a beautiful and loving moment and the wife innately knew that she was at home and safe. Her eyes exquisitely flickered... and at that moment the whole room lit up in a sign of hope.

Now, finally seeing his wife move, albeit very slightly, Kerisay Senior's heart was immensely buoyed, whereupon he hurriedly turned away, eagerly scooped up the sparklingly, delicious and fresh water in a cup from the bucket in the kitchen, which was replenished hourly from the family well, located just outside the front door.

With one dexterous move, he gently and tenderly guided his wife's head and the son placed a soft pillow under his mother's head. She was peacefully resting on her side now, at an angle of forty-five degrees.

To administer the cool and refreshing liquid, he brought a drinking straw and placed it into the cup. The cup was in turn stationed on a low flat wheeled trolley.

This was serenely rolled up to Rolanda-Runa, who hearing the wooden wheels distinctly stutter and then emit a rather deep resonating sound, which only her floor could do, triggered the opening of her eyes in full. She proceeded to take a few sips of the vaguely blueish coloured water via the straw, which caused her to bow her head in approval and calmly smile simultaneously.

"Rest my wife," pleaded Kerisay Senior, and with that he imperturbably laid a strong, warm, and durable blanket over her, a material sourced from cotton with the spun thread intricately interweaved, producing a spectacular rectangular-shaped blanket.

The father and his son left the room and stayed outside the house, admiring the sun setting... with the father wishing that he had decided to travel with his wife and had he done so, perhaps he could have ensured that circumstances would have been different. He felt terribly guilty, but he felt constrained in the presence of his son.

His wife was alive, but it would take time for her to recover completely and he sensed, like his son that perhaps their world was changing.

Accordingly, there was an inkling that amplifying quietness, furnishing mannerisms of developing introversion, projected by his son, would have to be resolved.

Chapter 4 - Rolanda-Runa Absorbs the Dream

Time passed seamlessly by, certainly from the perspective of the capybara world. More so, after the epochal defining and dreadfully horrible storm.

It was now the 9th of May.

Yet, though a tumultuously dangerous event had occurred, precisely two weeks ago that had shaken the north-west of the capybara island, one matter remained and was indisputable. Rolanda-Runa was an amazingly gifted capybara — with an inborn common sense and astute logic encapsulating every decision she made.

Needless to say, though palpable facts about the source of the nightmare remained opaque, Rolanda-Runa instinctively recognised that the danger could reappear and worsen her world. She further hypothesised the importance of keeping any ideas under wraps, as she distrusted the C-Echelons, who lived in a surreal world most of the time, with their spies. Yet there was the need to also resolve her son's predicament, which she could gradually sense would need addressing.

Finally, as the days elapsed, there was a growingly grave realisation that a negative force, unknown in recent decades, had glaringly pierced the idyllic world she inhabited. Certainly, there was a feeling of undisclosed information and this immeasurably troubled her.

Nevertheless, she fiercely protected her family and recognised that this protection was prerequisite.

Her husband and son were prevented from fleeing the family home, but perhaps this was lady luck's intervention. Rolanda-Runa's husband could and would naturally protect her, shielding her from prying eyes in their newly built basement, to help her completely recover from the shocking experience, which had severely jolted her. Yet, it only required one slip-up about her situation, for word to leak out to the leadership and the family would face insurmountable pressure to pay for care and an "investigation".

It is worth pointing out that there were refuges, which provided shelter for the poor, weak and vulnerable, who could not remain in their family home, but these refuges were overseen, by the self-indulgent C-Echelons, who extracted a punishing heavy price from the family. Of course, these places were a non-starter to many from a perspective of dignity and finance.

There was an expectation that Rolanda-Runa would improve, regardless of the severity of the event, as she was such a tour de force, a force of nature, a giant of a personality complemented in no small measure, with a dignified virtue that encapsulated her whole being. To be close at hand, when Rolanda-Runa returned was also a heaven-sent gift for her immediate family, as spirits were undeniably lifted and hopes raised by all those concerned.

Assuredly, as alluded to, life in many ways now plodded on fatefully, since there was a feeling that life must go on.

Regardless, a more damaging misconception was that a repeating catastrophe, with a calculated and compound vengeance was seemingly for the future! This was not just a passing thought from a few capybaras, but a perception from the entire community, including the C-Echelons.

The C-Echelons were simply not averse in past travails to sweep things under the carpet, let sleeping dogs lie, and let their bygones be bygones. The pretentious and absurdly austere C-Echelons were not entirely interested in the community, but liked to feather their own soft, food-laden, and luxurious nests. Their penchant was to dress in long, flowing purple robes (the more important the rank the deeper the purple colour would be), plus purple t-shirts and trousers, added to the pervasive and rather incongruous wearing of a purple bow tie. They were purveyors of self-serving deeds, visions of grandeur and self-importance.

But this new situation that stormed the island was a matter, which could not be ultimately ignored.

In any degree, dutiful Rolanda-Runa improved incrementally, which synchronously saw time effortlessly pass. She proceeded to very slowly plan her re-engagement with the community, through assisting vulnerable and isolated capybaras with food deliveries. At ground level, there was need to repair, support and rebuild the society, which she was determined to eventually partake in.

Work was never done in half measures by the capybaras — the exceptions being the C-Echelons, who were viewed increasingly as being pampered, aloof, and out of touch.

Whilst this rebuilding process progressed on the island, the negative energy force had been reflecting for a while in solitude, on how its vassal storm had seemingly faltered, encountering a brick wall of positive loving energy emitted from a special capybara, whose activated magical prayers caused robust opposition.

The dark, negative energy force was furiously and insanely demanding that there would be no repeat and fascinatingly, the name Rolanda-Runa was unknown to the SSK1.

On the home front, Rolanda-Runa was displaying more self-confidence and mental fortitude. This coincided with her noticing that her son was growing unusually quieter by the day.

He was now strangely introverted and would spend time in the drawing room.

Whilst her husband, was busy juggling a work life balance, she decided to nip matters in the bud, with regards to her son.

Determined to raise the introverted matter with her son, she recognised that though they were growing communal concerns and distractions outside the home that needed time and patience to resolve, her family required to be prioritised.

Besides, there was no time to lose and speaking to her son was deemed a pressing issue.

Yet, her conscience kept plucking away at her heart strings, as she had also noticed how other capybaras had been deeply disturbed by the recent dreadful events and she was providing counselling to them.

Then, those she loved the most would induce realism and a greater desire to help her son. Though, her son had always been vocal, and enthusiastic about even the most mundane of matters, his demeanour was not positive. So, on this perfectly sunny and warm afternoon, she addressed the matter head-on with him about the disquiet, which was filling his mind.

"My son, what is the matter?"

"Nothing mother... everything is absolutely fine!"

"I'm glad I can speak to you in the drawing room. You've been very, very... subdued in recent days. Normally you are the life and soul of the party," she added jokingly, with the gentlest of reassuring smiles, trying to tenderly lift his spirits.

"SERIOUSLY mother... please stop the questions," was the gloomy, frustrated, and exasperated response.

"I do care son and... care so very much. You can always speak to me, you know. I love you."

At this point in proceedings, Rolanda-Runa thought about how she might cheer her son up and more poignantly determine if she could remedy an impending problem, which she sensed was brewing. Having that intrinsic ability to recognise that an issue was playing on her son's mind, she considered how best to approach his mood.

Remedially positive spellbinding songs, which were always at the tips of her unusually short, yet surprisingly dexterous fingers. She began to deliver the following first tune, comprising of two quatrain verses, which she called *Life*. The process was completed by *A Silver Lining* melody that possessed soothing rhyming and uplifting couplets.

Life, LIFE, life, life,
Can be truly amazing.
Love, LOVE, love, love,
Can be beautifully crazy.

Life, LIFE, life, life,
Is so cherishingly simple.
Love, LOVE, love, love,
Caresses a radiant sky.

A silver lining, lines each, and every cloud,
"Don't be sad," I'll proudly say out loud.

Life may not be straightforward at times,
But our hearts are so entwined.

If you encounter a mental haze,
"Tell me... with haste," I'll say unfazed.

"I can protect you," I'll proclaim,
Like the fiercest lion, maned, untamed.

As the purest of pure blue skies,
Serenade the clouds for endless miles,

There will never be anything,
That I can't help; I repel with a mental sting.

After a lengthy pause, the young son began to cogitate. The mother could see that perhaps the songs had an impact.

"Mother, there is something that is bothering me!"

"Speak my son."

"Well mother, when we thankfully found you late on the 25th of April, I was relatively fine at first. Then, by the 2nd of May, the dream suddenly was aroused. It is now the 9th of May and I am really worried!"

"Tell me more Kerisay?"

"Well, I'm concerned about the welfare of a new friend.

"Go on," gently encouraged the mother.

"The dream's a repeating one and is set in a different world. A friend of mine shall seemingly disappear and I'm wondering, if this is a sign of foreboding danger. I can't relinquish the dream, the shadows, or the troubling humming of the landing mirror and by the end of the day its making me sadder!"

"My son, I will help with this type of dream, which I know of! What I will do now, you must never tell to anyone, including your father. I was prohibited from using one particular gift in the open, but I cannot sit idly by and see your suffering!"

"I don't understand mother?"

"Listen, my beloved son to what I will say. Trust in me. Have faith in our gods. I am going to pray. I have just one red bead left and the special prayer will relieve you of the dream. When I have a wish, it will come to fruition."

Rolanda-Runa did not tell her son that though he will be saved, she may suffer.

Intriguingly, she also would avoid explicitly using the word spell and instead make reference to a prayer or poem that would appear to implicitly trigger an intercession with the gods.

"But... what will happen to me and more importantly to you?" enquired a shocked Kerisay.

"You will fall asleep my son and your negative dream will be passed to me. There will be no long-term effects. Then I shall be able to address the dream and resolve this. Once there is a resolution, the replay button of the dream will be extinguished."

"Is it safe?"

"Yes… and you will be assisted, my love. Do you understand what I am telling you?"

"I understand, mother."

"Good. Please close your eyes and let us stand together."

Divine spirit that transfuses our island world,
Shine the godly light, transmit and unfurl.
Allow me to receive my son's dream,
Come into my heart and gleam.

Protect my son and the island from any harm.
Stop the negative dream and bring him calm.
A silent whisper to you my son I shall send,
Learn later that my dream shall transcend.

Withal, protect north-west region,
Let me harness strength and be a legion,
Shield my son; let my spell flow,
Have awareness of what I know.

So, protect my family, my beloved son,
Then, return me home, be at peace, to have won.
Thus, my family can reunite,
I plead for hope, salvation, a breather, and respite.

Now, bring him respite,
With haste and speed.
Take this dream!
Be my torchbearer, allow his heart to gleam.

At this juncture, as the son began to feel drowsy, the final red bead that the mother held disintegrated and a crackle could be heard, which was resoundingly discordant, and immediately the son fell off to sleep, peacefully.

The mother left the room, walked towards the first-floor library, and five minutes later, departed the library and headed to the magical, sturdy wooden mirror, which was located in close proximity to the stairs. She entered this beautifully decorated and rectangular mirror and then... vanished.

Soon afterwards, Kerisay woke up in a daze and greatly alarmed. Though, a tormented weight had been undeniably lifted from his melancholy shoulders, he was instinctively worried about his mother. He was constantly fidgeting.

"Where could she be? Where could she be?" he fearfully, repetitively and nervously contemplated.

The replay button of the never-ending dream ceased, yet he felt that he had temporarily endured a kind of knowledge gap. Add to this fact, an extraordinary tiredness was detrimentally all-consuming.

From the mother's perspective, she recognised time was prerequisite and to impart too much knowledge on her son, who could get quite emotional, would be counterproductive and lead to possibly negative consequences.

Without doubt, the son and mother were now in different worlds. The son would, for a while at least, struggle to remember key timeframes and just be consumed, with a loving reminisce of his mother's enduring qualities.

Chapter 5 – The Island: A Loving Reminisce

The luxuriant dining room table cloth was an exquisite, rich sea blue, which mirrored the unique hue of this particular world's forbidden only known sea. The wonderfully crafted Java kapok dining table was literally adorned, with several beautifully framed upright pictures, illustrating a broadly smiling female capybara standing against the mantelpiece, elegantly wearing her favourite yellow hat, with pink and red ribbons.

Situated elegantly on the mantelpiece was a beautiful light brown, wooden clock that had been finely and honourably crafted (it was told) by the benevolent and celebrated President's craftsmen, as a tribute to the family's devotion, and each of the twenty-four numbered hours on the surface of the clock was coloured in sparkling turquoise that reflected the magnificent colour of this planetary, lower gravity world located in the extraordinary Solar System ZA123-123B.

Although, no creature had ever seen the President, there was a discussion that this was just made up to keep the capybaras in control. Perhaps she was just an imaginary figurehead established by the C-Echelons to keep the animal's content?

On the clock, the day and year appeared in bold font, whereby each character had been expertly printed on top of small, white rectangular plastic strips. The long date for this exoplanet stated: Wednesday, 11th May 2163. It was lunchtime and the phrase, Phase Two nestled neatly under the long date.

In this unique rodent world, a day would be divided into three unique periods called Phases, with each period lasting precisely eight hours.

The first eight hours would be Phase One and would encompass the sleeping zone. Generally, individuals would wake up at precisely 08:00 (oh eight hundred hours) and it took at least forty-five minutes for them to be prepared for any activity that would follow.

The middle Phase or Phase Two would encompass a further 8 hours that would cover the events for the day, when young individuals would attend a local school, do homework and undertake competitive sporting activities, plus partake in family chores, whereas the elders would be working industriously at a nearby location, for much of that middle Phase.

The last third (or ending Phase), better known as Phase Three, would be time spent with family and friends, shopping, and casually playing leisurely sports and end precisely at 24:00 (twenty-four hundred hours), five hours after sunset.

Phase Three, was the one loved most by capybaras.

Each hour would last sixty seconds, or sixty-one for the C-Echelons. It is worth pointing out that from an astronomical perspective, the extraordinary planetary world of the capybaras would take 360 days to rotate around the Sun.

Nonetheless, the focus in the dining room, was undoubtedly on the countenance of the genial individual, who was a wife and a mother, with adorably deep, brown, marginally elongated eyes that were serenely gazing at the heavenly of the heavenliest sky. She was wearing a stylishly beautiful scarf, red coloured, around her bristly fur neck that concealed the wearing of her coloured beads adorning an elegant necklace.

In the portrait's background was the magnificently majestic Round Ringed Rodent Outer River (RRRO River), which was elevated 3 metres above the Ring Moat. The RRRO River stretched for 28.26 miles, was 3 metres at its deepest (0.3 metres in the shallows), one mile wide, and was emphatically circular in design.

But the incredible RRRO River had at strategic points, in the north, south, east, and west, a parallel circular inner ring tributary river (with the same width and depth dimensions, as the outer ring), which would automatically replenish the major outer one. Between the outer and inner rings, the water filled moat had an area of 25.12 square miles.

How this amazing design came about was a mystery to the new generation of capybaras.

Nonetheless, the outer-ring was perceived as a useful defence mechanism against some of the massive, least friendly, and more antagonistic creatures that lived beyond the RRRO River and in particular on an adjacent island.

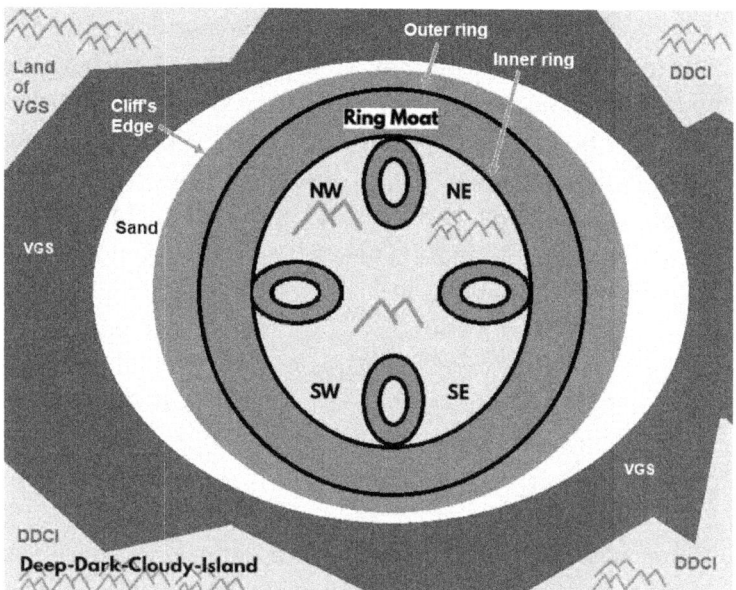

Anyhow, the female's short and thickset front and back feet were amazingly strong and slightly webbed; in fact, she possessed four toes on each of the two front feet, whereas three toes on each of her two back feet. In addition, her fur colour had a rich, light brown colour, but retained blue striations along the forearm, which led inexorably to the feet.

Certainly, at one time (as already alluded to), this capybara was immensely powerful and could also, majestically stand tall in the shallower parts of all the rivers and peer out at the horizon.

As with other creatures from this capybara world, the females liked to either wear sleeveless bright yellow or pink coloured blouses, plus baggy grey trousers, which tended to be rather worn at the end (a characteristic both males and females shared, when it came to their trousers' attire). In contrast, the males tended to wear pristine-looking white t-shirts, covered with an assortment of two-dimensional shades of blue shapes, accompanied with olive-green coloured trousers.

Indeed, specific north-west male and female creatures preferred walking upright, which made them impressive looking. Capybaras in this world grew to a maximum of one hundred and thirty-three centimetres from head to toe.

There was also a penchant of these animals to utilise their versatile front feet like hands to politely gesture and wave. Noticeably, these mannerisms did not endear them to the C-Echelons, who would find all of this to be problematic.

To all human readers, it is worth addressing the salient point that capybaras in this world, were not typically like the ones seen on planet Earth. Certainly, in the Island World of the Capybaras, their "hands" were incredibly useful and could be unexpectedly extended forward. Therefore, more skilful work requirements could be undertaken.

What was just as extraordinary was the longevity of capybaras.

Swiftly, returning back to the north-west region of the capybaras. Sometimes, these animals would gallop on all fours, if they were playing their version of non-combat soccer, where they would have to move around opposing players, nudging the football in the direction of the opposite goal.

Nonetheless, all capybaras regardless of their region were indefatigable and would be constantly on the go. They would never stop. If it meant ploughing the fields, planting crops, cleaning the roads, working in a shop or office, constructing a new building, or in their spacious homes painting and decorating.

The only pause was on a Day of Reflection when there was a remembrance for other capybaras, who had passed away or had gone strangely missing, or their whereabouts were unknown.

The reflective days would typically be held on a Wednesday, when capybaras (from across all regions) were not constrained by regulations. An alternative to the Day of Reflection, would be to consider undertaking charitable work.

All the other days of the week, especially over the weekend, normally witnessed an End Phase smorgasbord, whereby older relatives would visit one another for the sole purposes of eating and occasionally use the given occasion to discuss their work plans and ambitions.

If there had to be an event day, then a Saturday would be allocated.

For all capybaras, the structure of the week had been designed, according to the directives of the preening C-Echelons, since "time immemorial". This was the message that leadership bragged, blathered and crowed eternally about.

It is worth adding that work for the older capybaras was a source of great pride.

The quicker the job was completed; the individual would earn merit points from their employer and for the immediate family.

Typically, this would have a cumulative effect and mean that by the end of the year, the family could go away to the mountainous region and enjoy the wonderful clean air, extraordinary scenery and an amazing camping expedition.

Anyhow, in Rolanda-Runa's home, on the dining room table, three large, circular and chequered-styled edible plates (made of dough) were expertly placed and the distinctive bronze and gold squares were conjured from a sophisticated food colouring technique.

The squares were layered diagonally in a wonderful pattern, across the surface of the plates, enticing the daylight.

Collectively, the gold squares glistened majestically as the massive Sun's summer rays first scanned and then circumnavigated the circumference of the plates, as if trying to identify the most pertinent location to nestle down and then at an instance, like the flick of a switch, it appeared to cradle with deliberate circular motions, the outer contours of the plate with such precise and infinite care; abetted with a flickering and soft gentleness, almost like a doting mother would lovingly care for her baby.

In fact, the very large edible plates were precisely and marvellously ten point five inches apart, no more and no less, from each other.

A hand-knitted napkin (with a lime fragrant) was located across each one of the plates and folded expertly. Emblazoned majestically on the napkin was the name Rolonda-Runa.

At the top of each plate, there was a deliberate and slight cosmetic scratch, hardly noticeable to the naked eye. To the right of the scratch, located at ten degrees and five seconds, was a large, chilled glass of water perfectly positioned.

The spectacular silver cutlery glistened and looked almost new, as they would be polished for an inordinate amount of time. A shiny metal knife was placed to the right of the plate, a fork to the left of the plate, and a further right of the knife was a large cereal spoon.

A couple of metres away, the sound from what appeared to be two handsome-looking capybaras preparing a sumptuous Day of Reflection meal, could be heard in the busy, bustling, round, and sparkling adjacent kitchen.

They respected the occasion, as well as revered the countless pictures of the smiling Rolanda-Runa. They were honouring her, the demeanour she espoused, as well as her uniquely refined table etiquette.

As a consequence, they were enthusiastically attempting to conjure up the perfect meal in her recognition.

Each individual vegetable food item (with an intricately carved and tiny capybara face mark) had been placed precisely and intentionally, within certain squares on the circular plate to reflect an unbelievable chess board scenario.

Four of each of the following (two white coloured and two purple coloured): tomatoes to indicate the bishops, shortened squat-shaped celery pieces to reflect the castles, and triangular-shaped sliced cucumber portions representing horses, were positioned precisely in the middle of each of the bottom and top two rows of the plate, mirroring its opposite location, reminiscent of how a board game with chess pieces would respectively be positioned and ready for a battle to the "death".

Interestingly, eight white mushrooms would be positioned from A2 to H2 and eight purple mushrooms located between A7 to H7. There were two white radishes as well as two purple radishes, each representing the respective kings and queens.

Besides, the edible gameboard, they were preparing the sumptuous lunch to include, finely sliced boiled portions of succulent melons on toast, as well as an assortment of colourful wheat cereal flake shapes, covered with deliciously cold, full-cream milk.

The slices of toast had been just prepared and were heart-warmingly warm, a luscious brown colour and evenly grilled to perfection, and covered with delicious slices of ripe, juicy, and succulent apples (without seeds of course).

All in all, the food was beautifully spread out on the dining table.

In this unique world of mostly cuddly looking, sociable, mainly effervescent capybaras, the father and his son Kerisay were trying to forget their tears and remain upbeat, after enduring the sudden disappearance of Rolanda-Runa.

To that extent, the father and his beloved son were concentrating on preparing the most majestic food.

They were undeniably close and very much like friends, plus there was a mutual respect.

The meal preparation, was their way to cope and distract their great worry from the all-consuming sadness that filled every corner of their heart.

At this point in time, the father was doing most of the talking and directing his son, who carried out his duties quietly and meticulously, which was not normally how he would approach work of this nature.

Customarily, on a Day of Reflection, those making a special meal in honour of the individual, would each need to recite a poem, with the eldest family member speaking first, who would refer to the missing individual for example.

The father though, wished to carry out this requirement on his own, as his son was in a deeply pensive mood.

Thus, Kerisay Senior adjusted his clothing to suggest he would soon be reading both poems out.

Incidentally, the first poem concerning his wife Rolanda-Runa, had been planned to be delivered with an emphasis on the syllables and then the second poem that his son had penned, to be voiced in quick succession, presenting a distinctive requirement to provide attention to the end of line rhyming words.

Both poems were intended to be very moving, reflecting the deep love the family had for Rolanda-Runa.

Still, for capybaras, even in the north-west region and with the knowledge transfer subconsciously passed, remembering a poem verbatim, less so formulating one, was not straightforward at all.

If the mind was not fully focused, it could take the proverbial blood, sweat and tears to finally implement!

Work of this nature, took a great deal of patience for those who did not have the gift like Rolanda-Runa.

"I will undertake the poems slowly my son," clarified the father.

"No problem father, I will be glad to hear them. The second poem was constructed hastily, but hopefully... you will like it!"

"I am sure I will. This whole process is cathartic. Before I forget, I really wanted to say this... about the poems. I have cut corners. To be honest, neither of us is in a position to remember the poems, so I have written them down. The first poem, is very evocative."

"Without a shadow of a doubt. Also, the poems father, will help us remember."

"Yes, that's true. By the way, thank you, my son for your excellent contribution with the second poem, which I'll never forget. Now, please listen, as one poem will follow another."

Poem 1

Her beauty will not fade but re- main strong.
Her hearty laugh shall not die as we live.
As we look above, we see the sky-line.

Her beauty rings out as the bells do throng.
Her he-arty hug be remembered re-live,
Rolonda-Runa you are so divine.

The laughter shall linger and be vivid;
The gentle- ness envelopes the home now.
As we look beyond the sky- line see hope.

We shall remember her days and spirit
Rolonda Runa remember, we bow;
Shall lift the mast colours be never taupe

Her gentleness out- shines everything.
Strength she possesses — insurmountable.
Dangers exist a-round, but she is brave.

And does show indefatigability.
Remorseless — she is a survivor,
Plus, will be no one's slave, never enslaved.

Poem 2

Mother dearest, how I miss *you*
And the gentle smile, the gentle *hug*,
When times are tough, I know what's *true*
You're in my heart, a love can't *shrug*.

You have an energy that is *pure*;
A devotion that can't be *overestimated*.
Even so, you're kind and *demure*,
But underneath, so *sophisticated*.

You are tireless and try to *help*,
Always giving and never *taking*,
Always smiling, yet never *yelp*.
Working, being strong, never *breaking*.

At home, here in the morning, just *Monday*,
But your now gone, to where I don't *know*.
This is a Day of Reflection, a sad *Wednesday*.
Next, deflect dark shadow, a no *show!*

You believed in no bad luck, no on button to *destruct*.
There's just your strength, no end *length*,
Amidst a determination to succeed, *construct*,
So, I'll help, find clues, no higher than the *10th*.

The father had overlooked his son's penultimate and final stanzas about a dark shadow and reference to the 10th respectfully, as his mind was in overdrive, considering pensively about where his wife could be and what predicament she may be in.

"I need to ask about the words and perhaps there is a hidden meaning?" the father analysed very quietly to himself.

"Excuse me father?"

"Sorry, just talking to myself. Would you like to expound what you have said my son?"

"I just said… instinctively what… had come… into… my head," was the son's intriguing, but slightly long and jittery riposte.

The father's desire to see his son smile again was an overriding concern, as he could recognise that his son's heart was truly aching, wanted releasing and did not wish to see the bleakness in the youngster's eyes. Talking was the best policy and he considered how a conversation could be initiated.

As they looked around the room, their minds forged telepathically to bolster their aspirations.

This prompted a precipitous calmness to descend, whereupon they uttered in a synchronised and controlled silence the following.

Though the crimson coloured flowers are sad,
In our home, we'll find a certain hope from
The clutches of despair.
Past memories can be surely reawakened,
Exploring, bringing a semblance of comfort,
To relinquish the cross, we bear.

"I know how you feel my dear Kerisay. Is there anything you would like to say or tell me?" enquired the father tenderly and with empathy, as he noticed his son, after a temporary pause of reflective silence, was still unusually quiet, too reticent (which was rather peculiar), as the youngster always had plenty to comment on.

Indeed, it was the son's idea to prepare the lunch precisely, since two tortuous days had elapsed since his mother's departure and a Day of Reflection would have to be initiated. A Day of Reflection would initiate a dialogue. This is what the father was aiming for.

"I miss mother so much and my heart aches. I am unsure... if I will ever see her again. I do not know when she will return?" tearfully exuded the young capybara, in a rhetorical manner.

His youthful appearance was still noticeably evident, among the tears streaming heavily down his face.

"We will find her, my dear son. But without her guiding light, life is just not the same is it?" was the emotional response.

These gentle and reflective words prompted the grey-whiskered father to approach his son, whereupon he hugged him warmly and reassuringly.

It was a light bulb moment. Suddenly, memories began first slowly in a trickle and then rapidly flooding back into Kerisay's mind. It was almost as if, the intense feelings of solitary sadness had blocked out recent key events. His father's loving reassurance, as well as the poetic words had awakened specific dormant memory cells within his mind.

"Father, I would like to talk about my dreams and then can I ask you a question?"

"Of course. Go ahead son… you are always able to speak freely."

"I can't say that my repetitive dream is an entirely contented one. I travel in time and though I may remember a joyful event in the dream's episode, when we lived in the famous capital, which was covered with one thousand acres of luscious grass and beautiful crimson coloured flowers, this dream is followed quickly by an abrupt end that is a real dangerous dampener on matters.

"Indeed, I keep on having the same dream for days on end. It is almost as if there was a gratuitous toying of my mind."

The father blinked his eyes to encourage his son to continue.

"Day after day, the dream was exactly the same and, on each occasion, it finally ended at a level of grave uncertainty. Truly, by the end of the week, it had not changed for the better.

"I spoke to mother and she said that for her, the dreams only end when she speaks to someone about what has happened. My dream feels as if they will lead to a terrible conclusion that will be a truly melancholy one. For a while, the same dream has taken place each and every day as per usual. I am really nervous about how it will finally all end and whether the dream is a precursor to a scary, or even foreboding event that will take place in the future."

"Where are you specifically in this particular dream Kerisay?"

"I'm witnessing the moment the guinea pig will soon disappear. By the way, has mother ever spoken about a charming guinea pig called Jettison?"

"Sorry, what is the name?" was the emphatic riposte.

"Jettison. His name... is Jettison."

"Oh, I see! Kerisay, we knew some guinea pigs in the past and they had all these amazing names and of course, when you were younger, one disappeared. I do have a vague recollection, about what your mother, my lovely Rolonda-Runa, thinks about guinea pigs. She likes them and as a matter of fact, loves all animals."

The father tended to waffle a little, but his momentum inspired him to carry on speaking.

"When you were a pup, she would bring amazing food from out of nowhere, an adorable guinea pig face would appear on the food. She maintained seeing others smile keeps her young. That ability to conjure things out of the air is your mother's gift and is quite honestly, far beyond understanding."

"Yes, the guinea pig is in the dream father. Well, the dream is perhaps at an interesting point, when the pup is showing his in-built inquisitiveness and at the moment, he appears to be leaving the safety of the home."

"That is most curious," retorted the father.

"I can imagine why mother would have an affection for these animals. But in this latest dream, there are the shadows of multiple hands, calling out to the pup, ushering him onwards and he follows them blindly."

"Oh, I see! That does not sound good at all," tensely replied the father, as the lines on his forehead narrowed and his eyes were focused on his son in a sign of complete concentration.

"Truth be told, I am unsure where Jettison will end up father," reflected the son further in a melancholy manner.

"Your mother told me she had heard of dream patterns with shadows and hands reaching out, my son."

"What... no father... I cannot believe it!"

"Your mother is powerful, can see things and is a survivor. In contrast, I am preoccupied with my work and perhaps she thinks I am uninterested in her life, so our conversation tends to end on mundane topics and is generally focused on your grandmother. It's not that I am uninterested in what your mother has to say; I had been so worried about your grandmother's health, and then she passed away just before the terrible storm."

The father enjoyed talking at length. He resumed.

"I have been asked by your mother, if I could look at an interesting silver folder of hers, but being hopeless, I would forget. Whereupon your mother would roll her eyes and show exasperation. I can't blame her. You see, by the evening I am completely exhausted and instantly, fall off to sleep!"

The son was struggling to come to terms with his father's implications, but thinking quickly on his feet his mind began to show signs of greater clarity.

Be that as it may, his father had more to say.

"My son, the dreams your mother recounted were frankly vague, as far as I was concerned. Her dream could be very gentle and brief at first. By the end of the week, the entire dream would have an ending... and your mother was reluctant to expound on what took place. She mentioned an energy form that caused misery."

"Oh, I see! May be that energy form has returned? My dream, I suppose is perhaps... a little different, yet still repetitive. Was one of the dreams she mentioned anything to do with a guinea pig called Jettison? Please think."

"Going back to the name of the guinea pig. This is strange... a strange phenomenon," countered the father in an abstract way, before proceeding.

"As your mother did not reveal all of the dreams, I cannot say for certain whether or not Jettison appeared in them. But first, you must tell me all about your dream in full and transmit this... please."

The father was well aware that his wife, when they first got married, had made reference to Jettison, as a family friend. Hitherto, there had not been a need to delve deeper into this.

Jettison had been a handsome capybara, but an eternal, anti-aging potion he was developing, went horribly awry. It was believed that a dark energy force had been commissioned to punish the "miscreant" Jettison, whose appearance drastically altered and in distress he fled, never to be seen again.

"Okay, father. Over the course of last week, the entire dream was initially in little snippets and began gently, and then the length of the dream developed and extended, so more information was revealed. Finally, Jettison arrived.

"Having said that, the situation dramatically changes and by last Sunday, the guinea pig begins following these idiosyncratic shadows. I can't help but think that the distressing shadows are luring the animal to who knows where and possibly the shadows belong to a creature from another world, whom I have never seen before… and then the dream promptly ends," Kerisay remarked in a matter of fact manner that brought a sparkle of interest to his father's eyes, who was displaying enthusiasm.

"That is not every aspect of the dream or the transmission… is it? The full details of the dream I need to hear and should be conveyed please."

"Yes, I do understand. I will concentrate more. This is what… happened father."

Expeditiously together, the father and son walked up to the dining room table, then instantly sat down facing each other.

The food on display in front of them appeared truly amazing and the mother would have been proud of how meticulously her son and her husband had prepared the food full of nutrients.

As the young son gazed in admiration at his father, he was able to transmit his thoughts clearly and at an instance.

The content was fully absorbed by his father with what just looked like a single concluding blink of two eyes.

What is more, the telepathic process first began, when the son opened and closed his left eye and then his father reciprocated with his right eye, opening and closing it in quick succession, to synchronise the transmission of information.

Lastly, the father closed both eyes to switch off the transmission and opened them rapidly, so the eyes looked like they had blinked.

A few seconds elapsed. Next, the father closed his eyes tightly in deep concentration, as if the dream transmission had been locked away securely in his mind.

As the father's eyes began gradually opening, the content of the message was fully understood and the son's revelatory dream transmission began to be analysed by the father in upmost silence.

The mental transmission thus occurred, which does follow in the next chapter, with alacrity and in totality within a relatively small-time frame.

Chapter 6 - The Dream's Transmission and Revelation

It was a wonderful and bright spring day. The year was surprisingly also 2163, in this strange world.

It was in fact, Monday 9th May at 3 pm to be more precise, in the admirable capital called Rolanda-Runa Town (in memory of the female founder, countless generations ago), located in the region north-west of the island.

Also, the place had developed from a small town into a much larger one, with sprawling shopping centres and amenities for young and old alike.

It was the third day of an unusually glorious month, especially when compared to the atrocious wet weather that had preceded it.

There was a clutch of joyful, white and cotton wool-shaped clouds that delicately and absentmindedly mingled in the delightful expanse of a luxurious azure coloured sky, with a couple of child-like clouds frolicking in their inimitable manner.

Now, the endearing two clouds looked like they were incessantly teasing each other by gently bumping into one another, to see which cloud was stronger.

Indeed, if one were to gaze intently long enough and focus exclusively on just these two child-like and joyously smiling clouds, one could really imagine them communicating and appearing to play in their own sky version of hide-and-seek.

The smaller, slightly more fragile looking and smiling cloud would hide behind a larger and more maternal one, whereas the second, smaller bustling, and slightly more energetic cloud, encompassing a greater number of dust particles, would leave the scene and subsequently, in a dramatic manner, appear and bounce back into the fray, from the corner of the sky in search of the cautious and smaller hidden one.

It was a picture of pure harmonious delight. It was a simply audacious and awe-inspiring wonder undertaken by the two small clouds, but the entire spectacle would lift any melancholy heart.

Moreover, the air was so refreshingly and enticingly vibrant, which made one feel like devouring the oxygen like a ravenous lion and more so, the entire ambience appeared thoroughly invigorating.

The newly cut and even grass outside the family home's front windows had been recently cultivated meticulously by the splendid gardener and was a wonderful sight to behold. The luscious green grass glistened magically amid determined rays of sunshine trying to break through and shower a lavish warmth and love on all that it surveyed; its immaculate rays of heavenly sunlight trickled down in radiant bursts of syncopated delight, rebounding onto the large Victorian like windows and the adjacent hexagonal paving stones (with alternate colours of fluorescent red and cloudy white) leading up to the elegantly imposing, heavy, slightly creaking and mahogany ash grey coloured front door, which conjured up quite a regal setting.

As the homeowner made her way towards the front gate of the beautiful ash grey coloured house, she smiled serenely, whereupon she walked purposefully towards her front door and placed the portable, foldable pet carrier, gently down on the doorstep. The carrier was made of fabric and had zipped openings, which made it practical for transporting small animals.

The mother, Mrs Rolonda-Runa Roulliesum (a descendant of the town's founder) turned the key and opened the front door with her right hand, slightly brushing her beautiful rainbow coloured necklace. She took a step back and paused, as she somehow had forgotten to open the front door telepathically.

Anyway, she graciously and automatically lifted the pet carrier towards her left arm, as she smiled in a sign of anticipated knowledge at the thought of her son's forthcoming reaction to her pet announcement.

"Guess what we have brought home," exclaimed the mother in a joyful tone, as she elegantly stood in the front entrance of the sprawling hallway.

"What's that?" bawled Kerisay, a youngster of primary school age, as he bounded towards his mother in heightened excitement.

"Well, it is always something you have wanted. Don't you think?"

"Let's see! Let's see. Can you show me mother? Can you?" the exalted youngster joyfully and repetitively extolled in his white t-shirt, displaying light and dark blue coloured two-dimensional shapes.

"It's in this pet carrier. Now, just... a moment... please."

The youngster was jumping up and down, amazed, enthralled, swinging his arms around in happiness like colourful windmill blades, whilst whooping with delight, waiting to further explode in reverie, as to how he would react to the surprise, since it was possible to observe the contours of a small animal.

"Steady on Kerisay, we don't want to make the guinea pig nervous?"

"It's a guinea pig mother?"

"Yes, of course."

"I want to see!" he roared in contentment.

As the pet carrier was gently unzipped, the youngster could see an adorable looking wide-eyed guinea pig, a little over 6 weeks old, with an angelic innocence.

"He is amazing mother!"

Mrs Roulliesum gently coaxed the pup out with loving words, "Come on darling, don't be nervous."

Her son was now excited beyond belief.

The pup tentatively moved forward and then trundled up to the lady, cradling his handsome face against her legs. Then at a stroke, he turned tail and darted back into the comfort and security of the pet carrier container.

"We don't have a name for the guinea pig?" enquired Mrs Roulliesum serenely.

"What about Zinckar-Zinckar?" pleaded Kerisay in a curious tone, with his right eyebrow raised.

"Yes... that is interesting," replied Mrs Roulliesum, who was focusing on the pup rather than the tone of her son's voice.

"Better still, Ninckar-Ninckar," added the son sarcastically, with his left eyebrow extravagantly uplifted.

"Perhaps... this is getting silly?" enquired the mother, who thought her son was not trying to be sincerely genuine and then in a sign of exasperation, slightly grumbled, "What about Zinckar-Ninckar?"

"Well... that will be a challenge to do!"

"That's it, we'll call him Zinckar-Ninckar!" emphasised the mother in a firm, but dulcet tone.

"NO, no, NO..., I was just kidding," agonisingly implored the young Kerisay.

"YES, yes, YES..., I am kidding dear Kerisay," was the robustly sweet response. *"But I do prefer Jettison."*

The youngster shrugged his shoulders, before protesting, "That is a peculiarly odd name."

"Undeniably, Jettison is a uniquely 'outlandish' name for a pet. It would be a paradox..., as I tend not to be nondescript, but I think this name... would generate considerable curiosity from the leadership and one particular recalcitrant individual."

The youngster was lost for words.

Quickly forgetting that he was more confused with the adult explanation, rather than having been deftly outwitted, which his mother was skilled at doing, he soon began thinking of the games that he could play with his new friend.

His mind was innocently overactive.

He particularly loved football, that is the television cartoon guinea pig version, but also had a penchant for reptilian football (which involved avatars that would vividly come to life in a four-dimensional world) and all sports in general.

He rushed back down the hall and scootered upstairs, two steps at a time, to the first-floor landing area. Next, he headed for the playroom to hurriedly write down the games he could play with Jettison. On route, he passed a mirror, which he always felt uncomfortable about. It always seemed to drone!

Soon, he was heading in the opposite direction, having collected what was needed from the bedroom.

Then, with a black biro pen and a sheet of A4 paper in hand, he rushed down the long and winding Victorian staircase, whereupon he landed on the ground floor with a purposeful thud.

Next, he turned a sharp left through the kitchen and dining room area, heading towards the majestic back garden. There was no stopping the youngster now, as game plans were being constructed.

Kerisay had exuberant ideas for challenging, fun, outdoor games, flooding through his mind like a tumultuous and riveting storm of excitement. The location for him, where the games could be played, would be in the wide expanse of the family garden, which was impressively massive.

The garden had a section that had activities that would make many a child green with envy: swings, a seesaw, a climbing frame, sandpit, and even a tent. The Java kapok trees that stood tall and proud at the back of the garden, as well as on either side, gave the ambience a certain physical stature.

Undoubtedly, the trees were imposing, to say the least, but also had a contrasting gravitas and delectable charm, plus a particularly wonderful stateliness with their hanging branches, which from a side view, collectively looked like a shock of hair that you may see exhibited by a musical rock star.

The seeming palatial character and atmosphere of the garden was a heavenly sight to behold. The trees' leaves had a fascinating texture and in shape were long and tapering, as well as being up to twenty centimetres in length. There was a lovely patio that formed an entrance into the garden and was used for dinner parties during the height of the summer season.

As a game starter, Kerisay thought of a maze with exits to heaps of food: hay, kale and pellets. The maze could be organised using slottable, transparent plastic panels that he could safely construct on the grass and make it look like an exciting activity.

The patio could be utilised as a grand entrance to the intended maze and the guinea pig could run around on the grass.

On reflection, when he calmed down, he considered that a little less of an ambitious approach would be more beneficial, reasonable, and straightforward. He thought of initially just stroking the guinea pig would suffice at this stage, to develop a trust between them.

There was undeniable nervousness on the part of the guinea pig pup. Indeed, gently holding the young boar would be more than adequate at this juncture, when playing with the new friend.

Kerisay, dreamily also thought about an off-the-shelf, 22nd century super deluxe pup playpen that would be a most appropriate acquisition, as the young animal needed to feed, exercise, feel safe, at ease, and comfortable.

On the other hand, it would be better if he showed that trust could be established with his new friend. This is what his mother would expect, as he noticed she was relaxing and happily reading a national newspaper, whilst gently sipping a piping hot cup of soothing mint tea that was perched on the elegant, wooden dining table. He would be gentle and friendly towards the guinea pig at first — that would impress her!

"Mother, how's Jettison?" chirped Kerisay.

"He's well dear and I can hear him munching on pellets inside the pet carrier container."

"Mother?"

"Yes dear, how can I help?" immediately replied the mother with a casual and gentle tone.

"Could we get a 'proper cage' for Jettison?"

"We have one already," the mother purposefully conveyed in a tone that was both soothing and angelic, before taking delight in divulging, *"It was supposed to be a secret. I will bring it... into the house in just a few moments. It's in the boot of the car."*

The mother was ever so, slightly distracted, as she was reading a wonderful broadsheet article about European princes and princesses.

Indeed, she loved reading about royalty and reminisced about her own childhood, when she saw a video of the beloved and wonderful Queen of England majestically walking past an ancient relative's house, during the 1977 Silver Jubilee celebrations.

"Really... that is great. It is so lovely. "That is wonderful mother. Thank you, thank you!" cheered the young son, whilst picturing the playpen in his mind.

"Just a second darling... let me get it for you!"

The mother promptly placed her newspaper down in one quick motion of fastidious simplicity.

It was done with bewildering and dexterous speed.

The corner of the current page being read was sweetly and expertly folded and then in the blink of an eye, the paper was folded again down the middle lengthwise. It was expertly done and the newspaper was tidily left in the top right-hand corner of the dining room table, as if it had been just delivered to the house, moments earlier.

"Can I come with you to the car?" enquired Kerisay in a gentle voice.

"Yes, of course, my son. We must remember to close the front door."

Kerisay and his mother departed the room holding hands. Around them were resplendent wildlife photographs from a recent island adventure, adorning almost the entire walled surface of the dining area. From there, they leisurely walked towards the austere hall, which was facing the winding staircase. On route, one framed picture, presented a wonderful and smiling guinea pig, which appeared surreal, with the animal's eyes hypnotically open, ready for its next spell!

"Mother, what made you get the new guinea pig?"

"Unexpectedly, my best friend gave the guinea pig to me after work today. She could no longer care for the little boar, because she was planning to migrate."

"Oh, I see mother. She must have been despondent?"

"Yes, she loved the animal, but unsurprisingly she felt truly guilty that she could not spend time and bond with him."

"Naturally," was the young son's immediate and emphatic response.

"These animals are social creatures and my friend's heart was breaking in two," the mother added in a measured and empathetic modulation, as she was trying to simultaneously turn the latch and open the front door with her right hand, whilst her son's right hand was gently being held in her left hand.

There was a respective nodding of mutual understanding, about the female friend.

By the front door, on the left-hand side of the hall there was a little recess in the wall, where the family would keep a glass display unit containing their favourite novels, and a little further forward, there was a small, dainty door stopper, which settled neatly and unobtrusively in the deep, blue carpet. Without consciously thinking, she adroitly collected the door stopper, sweeping it gracefully into the air and then proceeded to place the item near the hinge of the front door.

"That is really sad to hear about the guinea pig," reflectively observed Kerisay, with gentle silver teardrops welling up in his eyes.

The mother stopped and turned to her son and gazed lovingly into his eyes, in order to further explain and express her feelings about the circumstances concerning how she received the guinea pig.

"My dear and wonderful son. Yes... my friend was... between the proverbial devil and the deep blue sea. I felt terribly sorry for her.

"She spoke to me constantly and was pleading. Eventually, I just consented and she brought the guinea pig to the shop after work. She was naturally distraught, but what are friends for, but to help?"

Kerisay was absorbing each and every word spoken.

"Anyway, when Jettison saw me, he was nervous at first, and then when I picked him up and began feeding him food, he was happier and considerably calmer. He is an amazing guinea pig, popcorning, scootering around and he has the energy of a jack-in-the-box toy.

"Plus, he demonstrates his own distinctive personality, doesn't he? I couldn't help my son, but fall in love with the guinea pig and then bring him home. His eyes are irresistibly gorgeous, aren't they? They are delightful and innocent too!"

"I am so happy to have a pet as a friend," reflected the son.

"That's great! He's so cute and it is like a little halo hovers over his head, with cherubs flying about too."

"Yes, I see what you mean," retorted the son energetically.

"By the way, your father is still at work, and truth be told, at first, he was not so keen with the idea of a new pet, as we have had so many in the past and are constantly on the go, but then... when I sent him a picture of Jettison's joyful demeanour, his cold heart melted and warmed instantly at a stroke.

"In an instance, your father did not need any persuading at all, even going ahead to buy the playpen! He was hypnotised seeing Jettison running, displaying high-octane energy levels and the affection in Jettison's eyes, were reciprocated. What are your feelings about the guinea pig my son?"

By this time, Kerisay was preoccupied. He was delightfully hopping and playfully skipping to keep up with his mother's stride towards the crimson coloured family car and had his eyes fixed on the vehicle's car boot. In the euphoria of the moment, they had forgotten to secure the front door.

Unbeknown to Kerisay (whose heart would have been utterly crushed), Jettison had somehow sneaked out from the pet carrier container and was naively pursuing the humans towards the front door. The pup saw the front door open and a glint of sunlight caught its inquisitive eyes.

The recess of the wall presented a reflective shadow from the opposite side, where the shelves, containing bits and bobs, and notices hung on the facing wall, which made it appear very untidy. When the light shone down upon it, shadows sneakily appeared.

But there was some other activity going on in this recess, which appeared to be trying to get the attention of the pup and this was more sinister. In all intents and purposes, it looked like there were dark shapes resembling a collection of small individual hands ushering the boar away from the safety of his lovely new home and to the unexplored outside.

Oblivious to the peril, the young guinea pig took the opportunity to investigate the world beyond, with all its hidden dangers.

Hence, the curious pup tentatively moved forward, one unsteady paw at a time, and then peeped its head around the corner of the front door.

As the animal gazed from the safety of its new house to the outside, it took a gulp and a back step. But the enticing shadows were too persuasive and the pup trundled around the corner of the front door.

Automatically, the front door appeared to deliberately, slyly and surreptitiously close behind the pup.

Chapter 7 - The Dream's Analysis

The father now took a shocked step back and paused momentarily with a tear in his eye, as he was reminded of his beautiful wife's name, who had tragically to all intents and purposes disappeared, whereupon he hummed in a bewildered tone, before his queried observations.

"Isn't this a peculiar transmission? Also, tell me my son, at what time of the day did this new and specific dream sequence you had concerning the guinea pig begin?"

"It first took place at 09:00, at the beginning of last week, on Monday 2nd May. Immediately, after I woke up, I surprisingly entered a trance-like state and began to dream," promptly replied Kerisay.

"I see my son and the dream would be repeated at the same time every day? Is that right?"

"Frankly father, the dream would always start at the dot of 09:00 and be randomly repeated during the day, then continue, almost incessantly in that form throughout the week. I would enter a trance and it would take you or mother to speak to me, before I fully awoke. Yes, a familiar family voice would cause me to come out of the trance. Incidentally, at night, I would automatically sleepwalk in the direction of the mirror upstairs. It was as if someone was calling me."

"That's troubling to hear," the father pensively responded.

"Yes, it was troubling. Also, by the end of the week, on Sunday 8th May in the early hours of the day, when it was pitch black, I sleepwalked again, stood in front of the mirror and my eyes opened wide. I saw my reflection and then the reflection in the mirror disappeared and walked away briskly, as if it was annoyed. Then a new reflection appeared as if by magic that same Sunday but at night time."

"Oh, dear. Let me focus on one thing and be clear. Did you tell your mother about these matters? You also spoke about the dream's shadows?" the father's voice trailed off slightly as he had been momentarily distracted, due to becoming greatly enticed by the smell of splendid food.

"Yes, I did speak."

"Then what did your mother do?"

"Mother was determined to help and was of the firm opinion that she could make sure the dream ended happily and that the guinea pig would be rescued. So, she reassured me and then absorbed my last dream on Monday, 9th of May. Likewise, she repeatedly reflected how concerned she was about Jettison."

The father kindly gazed at his son in solemn silence. He felt his son had shown resilience in the face of adversity and this filled his heart with immeasurable pride.

"For good measure, mother articulated how she also wanted to find Jettison. She felt that Jettison had a connection to our family, which was not explained! Then, she described that she would need to rest after absorbing the dream, mentioning how the process would leave her at her most vulnerable.

"Let me add. Whilst, she was speaking, I began to feel a little drowsy. Just before 5.45 pm, she said that she had to meet a friend and left the house. I fell off to sleep and slept incessantly, without interruption, peacefully until the next morning."

"Prior to this recent dream you had, when was the previous one?"

"This is the first repetitive dream. As I said, it started on Monday 2nd May. They weren't bothersome at first, rather intriguing, whereupon they became repetitive and completely drowned out my other thoughts. By the 9th of May, the dream was truly overwhelming. I could witness every detail, but then this became scary!"

"This is incredible. Don't you think, this should have been conveyed to me much earlier?"

"I suppose so. Also, I knew you had lost your dear mother recently and my grandmother. Plus, I did not wish to burden you with the dream, as you also had so much on your plate, as well as the worry about the new job. Times are very tough, especially with the C-Echelons suggesting even more taxes."

"That is understanding of you, which I appreciate. I am truly grateful to you for thinking of me my son," reflected the father thoughtfully and compassionately.

"Going back to the recent dream ... I would like to continue."

"By all means. Go on Kerisay."

"Well, I sincerely believe mother was trying to help. Anyway, this very morning, Wednesday 11th, I got up from sleep and she was not in the house. She had vanished into thin air. I panicked. My mind was confused and there were key moments that were missing from my memory. I knew you have been busy in recent days, trying to adjust to the demands of the new job, and then later, I appreciate that you would be, in the adjacent village, after work, trying to arrange my maternal grandmother's funeral.

"Honestly, I have been really perplexed and I thought mother had also left yesterday morning to help out with the administration side of things concerning grandmother's funeral, because I'm aware that the C-Echelons expected a burial payment."

"Tell me, in what sense do you mean absorbed, and how was that manifested for you?" pondered the father, more curious by the second.

"The whole dream vanished from my mind at an instant. Mother peacefully sat down next to me in the drawing room and placed her hands on my forehead and spoke."

"After a few words, I began to feel drowsy. There were unusual colours and sounds that bounded around my room and appeared to rebound in every corner of my mind. I could hear mother telling me not to worry, as there would be no need for anxiety. Slowly, I felt her words had borne fruit, as I could no longer remember any detail of the dream.

"It was a blur when trying to recollect and then it disappeared. I realised then and there, that she had absorbed my dream on Monday 9th. Shortly later, I fell off soundly to sleep, but subsequently felt a knowledge gap. In the days leading up to the mysterious absorption process, it has been a monumental struggle to maintain my sanity."

The father sympathised with his son's strong emotions.

"Nonetheless, when I awoke this morning, as I said, she was gone, but I still felt strangely dizzy and physically weak too. Since then, I have been getting unusual feelings, every hour, as my mind from time to time, has been going blank waiting for information. I would repeatedly and briefly doze off and then awaken, as if part of my mind was receiving intermittent messages from mother."

The father responded by adjusting his t-shirt, which helped him to concentrate more.

"This communication would trigger a mystical sensation, whereby a door was being closed and suddenly my mind was filled with messages. Then it all began to make more sense. I began receiving stronger information from mother. What she conveyed was so incredible, but I needed to be extra careful. Very careful. I was unsure what she meant about this."

"I do see, I do see," replied the father in a rhythmic manner.

"As expected, she wanted me to show mental strength and control," the young capybara assured, before resuming at greater length.

"Yet, these new messages, some two-way with mother, demonstrated how terribly worried and stressed she had become, especially when telepathically she learned that my reflection disappeared in the mirror. She acknowledged that she had heard of dreams like mine, when she was my age.

"She added that when the first reflection disappears and a new one appears, you have to address the dream. Your mind is asking for help! The more reflections you see and walk away from, without them being addressed will mean that you will eventually grow frailer with every day that passes. There will be a sense of a strange irreversible guilt!"

"Remember, don't ever feel guilty Kerisay. You are amazing!"

Acknowledging the words of support, the son gently moved his head, before delineating, "She has, in her frequent bursts of transmissions, also addressed important issues, plus told me how she effortlessly walked through the upstairs landing mirror. She later overcame challenges that had been established by her... ancestor."

"The mirror! Oh, my goodness. Go on son."

"So, father, the mirror opened a special passageway. She progressed, eventually arriving in a strange world, inhabited by types of individuals, she had never seen before. A caveat. The challenges on route were hair-raising and one, in particular, required great skill.

"Following on from the immediate pathway through the mirror, what occurred next was truly sensational. It was almost as if, she was walking on air and then as she proceeded further into the darkness, it became pitch black in places; the ambience (which was calling out to her), made way for a thick foggy air that encapsulated her — shielded our world.

"Then, within a few seconds, the fog momentarily retreated to allow her to exit, due... to a determined perseverance to succeed. Straightway and in the line of vision, there were hundreds of crimson coloured wooden hatches with numbers or letters, or alphanumeric types on the front of the hatches."

"This is extraordinary," reflected the father.

"I concur. The sheer volume of hatches was awfully imposing. Some letters and numbers were upside down. Many hatches had a combination of more letters than numbers, or vice-versa.

"The entire 'container' she walked into was a square-based pyramid. Above her head, in every conceivable location were hatches that looked similar in terms of size. Father, they floated around and then extraordinarily secured their position, after every ten seconds, even if they were at an angle. Then, the hatches would recommence the movement and rotate positions and never stay in the same location. Many of the hatches made a clattering noise and one particular hatch caught her attention.

"On closer inspection, there was a humble and slow hatch, with regards to its appearance and movement respectively. This hatch had a silver number 3 emblazoned, on a dark coloured background. You know father, the number 3, is of course our house number on this island (but, I am unclear of the correlation). She proceeded to pull at a round handle, which had a plain silver hue, causing the hatch to open, whereupon a ladder dropped down. All the hatches had a colour design very much like the number 3 hatch."

"I am unsure, if we are out of depth here, but go on Kerisay."

"Bizarrely father, she climbed up the ladder, since the hatch was located above her, so it appeared, as if she was walking towards the ceiling. As she climbed up the ladder and further forward, it started to move from a vertical position to a horizontal one. The ladder slid forward and she clung on tightly, as if her life depended upon it. It transported her into a void of darkness. Behind her, the hatch door closed.

"Next, the ladder steadied and she could... proceed," the son deliberated.

"I am all ears, continue... Kerisay."

"After approximately ten minutes of walking forward, she finally could see the entrance to a different world, which was through the exit of a massive Java kapok tree facing a beautiful house (just beyond the luscious fields of long grass). The ash grey coloured front door of the house had a large silver coloured 3, making it all the more interesting and appealing.

"Looking all around this new world, was fascinating — like ours in terms of temperature! Significantly, there were other strange creatures, which mother referred to as humans: walking, talking and driving peculiarly shaped vehicles.

"Notwithstanding, she noticed that as she walked further north, in the direction of the house's front door, her footsteps could astonishingly not be heard and she spoke about being an apparition."

Kerisay Senior was entranced by his son's account, which the son could sense.

The son portrayed, "She advanced breezily and, on the porch, she could see a plethora of lethargic guinea pigs moving listlessly around their respective cages. All the cages were far too small for comfort, actually unnecessarily cluttered and lacking in basic hygiene.

"As she drew even closer, she noticed the animals were perhaps a little bigger than she had anticipated, but one approached her and voiced the sadness in his melancholy heart. He said his name was Jettison and described the state of his dreadful captivity."

"It's heart breaking to hear about the animals, my son."

"Absolutely. Disturbingly, the other guinea pigs looked very frail and in poor condition and they appeared very close to passing away; they also bitterly complained that their preference would be to socialise with others of their kind more often and had been living in the prison cells far too long. Before father time caught up with them, they would be constantly biting the frame of the metal cage to escape their dreadful incarceration."

"They would understandably have complained about the lack of space?" emotionally understated the father.

"Yes, and Jettison was fearful that he would end up being sold to a different owner. They had no real life!

"After a while, mother could hear familiar voices emanating from within that house. She was a little apprehensive, but heard the name Kerisay being called out. She then proceeded to float into the house and to her utter astonishment, she could see someone extolling the same characteristics as herself, speaking in the same tone and wearing clothes distinctly and spookily similar.

"This was an apparent human version of my mother, who also by the way wore a necklace made of the same rainbow coloured beads, plus a red coloured scarf that only mother would wear. This human was struggling financially to make ends meet and this had overtaken the necessity of caring for the guinea pigs.

"Withal, she was not of course the same in terms of youthfulness, or the same species for that matter, but older and looked frail for a human, when compared to the other people, who had been seen driving in their vehicles. This specific human female spoke sadly of the recent and unexpected passing away of her husband Kerisay Senior."

The father was flabbergasted with what he had heard and the detailed content conveyed was sheer mind-boggling and the last sentence was most upsetting to say the least.

It prompted him to intervene without any further hesitation, "Let me take this important information in… and cogitate…".

There was a little deliberation and he stretched his neck, as if acknowledging that he had been seriously affected by what had been relayed.

Before further proceeding, the father readjusted his t-shirt to complain, "But and this is a big BUT, my son, you really should have spoken to me earlier. My work could have waited. Anyway, I did not want to interrupt your flow."

"Yes, I do appreciate this… and I am sorry," before hastily continuing "also, mother was shocked by her old human appearance and what she learned!"

"This must have caused a reaction?"

"Agreed, and also the condition of Jettison did really unnerve her and I have never felt mother's emotions so on edge.

"In any case, she told me in a further transmitted message, which I just about caught the gist of, whilst I was in the process of dozing off again that she hoped to return later to the human world, but wanted to come home to see us. Travelling in time had made her horrendously weary. But she was determined to rescue Jettison, after she had spoken to the guinea pig. This was the last I heard from her and there were no new messages. As there has been no new contact, I am worried."

"I am concerned... my son and there is an unpleasantly distressing emotion evolving; a real... fear that she is trapped in that strange human world. She should have returned by now," lamented the father in a breaking voice.

"How will we retrieve mother?"

"I am quite unsure. Also, the last thing I want is for us to blindly follow and get trapped there too. It will be a challenge for us... I think. Where there is a will, there will obviously be a way. Don't you agree?"

"Perhaps father. May be, she decided more had to be done in that human world?"

"I really don't know my son. To be frank, no clear leads in the house have been left, for us to pursue. She has a gift, which I think she inherited. But, I unsure from whom. I would need to carefully look through the library upstairs for more information.

"Your mother hinted that your maternal grandmother kept her work in secure metal boxes and they were scrupulously dated and meticulously placed in the library, which she was very protective of and did not want anyone to access! She has talked about the mirror, which needs investigating?" the father further deliberated expressively.

"We need to consolidate what we know father."

"Yes, I concur my son. Yet, I have never seen the work from your mother at first hand. More often than not, she remained tight-lipped about magical or wizardry matters. On one particular occasion, she spoke vaguely about some enchantment and then refused to say anymore. She remained quiet. Anyway, I would not want her to admit to a Freudian slip," opined the father in a reflectively humourous tone.

"Part of this is my fault that your mother did not always trust me. I am not known for keeping secrets and in the past, I have foolishly revealed small, magically abstract or family matters at parties, which enraged your mother so much. I promised in the future to be more prudent, but she was always reticent to tell me everything."

"That is in the past father. We need to think ahead!"

The father unconsciously rambled on, "Perhaps she also realised how hard I worked and how disconsolate I had become, due to my employment redundancy notice two months ago and thus she did not want to burden me. She was very considerate. Of course, I have only just started a new building job. But and this is a big BUT, with the C-Echelons, you never know how long your work will last, do you?"

The son shrugged his shoulders, to illustrate uncertainty.

"Nonetheless, putting two and two together, my intrinsic feeling is that the upstairs landing mirror could be used as a passageway? What do you think?"

"It is possible father."

"Perhaps, there is a time of the day, when we can use the mirror? If we can identify the spell to control or open the mirror, then I am absolutely certain we can find your mother and bring her back safely to our world."

Chapter 8 - The Library Search

"Without further ado, let's go to the library upstairs," the father enunciated.

"Great idea father and should we commence the search in the library?" retorted the young capybara excitedly.

"I expect so Kerisay. Anyway, we shall see!"

Just then, they heard a resounding knock on their front door.

Kerisay rushed towards the door and on opening it, to his great surprise he saw his best and most trusted friend Zerisoyah and her more reserved twin sister Merisoyah, standing a foot away (looking rather bored and uninterested).

Zerisoyah, was of a contemporary age to Kerisay, yet she was assured, naturally gifted and not introverted, like her sister.

Both young female capybaras were slim and would dream about being elegant ballet dancers (moving like graceful gazelles).

From an interesting perspective, though Zerisoyah spoke in a softer and gentler tone than Kerisay, her mind was as sharp (mentally speaking), as the sharpest edge of a razorblade.

"What's the matter Zerisoyah?"

"Can I come in? It's urgent!"

"Can it please wait. Do you have to… Zerisoyah?" stuttered Kerisay unceremoniously.

The young female capybara was taken aback by his unusual lack of chivalry.

"I am… I am sorry if it sounds curt, but my mother has disappeared and my father and I are trying to work out… where she may have gone."

"Yes, of course. I understand… my friend. I am here, because it is to do with your mother's disappearance," matter-of-factly responded Zerisoyah.

"Oh, my goodness. What do you mean? How do you know my mother has disappeared?"

"I shall explain everything."

"Please do Zerisoyah."

This prompted Zerisoyah to walk purposefully forward and in turn, she was politely directed to the living room by her friend, not before instructing her more sporting sister in colloquial terms to stay put.

"Sis, just hang in there!"

To which, her sister just rolled her eyes and remained just outside the front door.

Inside the friend's home, she had a keen sense that Kerisay was in a hurry and required help urgently. She did not wish to mince her words and began to speak quickly and with great energy.

"My friend Kerisay, I was left warning messages by your mother. In these sombre messages, your mother explains that she is in a different world. It is a human one and it is not actually safe. The Earth year is 2163 and there are so many issues taking place. They have had terrible viruses, which have not entirely disappeared, plus there are constant wars and now there is the threat of a nuclear conflagration, between major countries.

"Unbelievably, some humans believe they can colonise a planet called Mars in their Solar System, which they believe is uninhabited, whilst they destroy their own planet!

"Sadly, the relationship between humans and animals is not entirely peaceful either. There are some animals exploited and in danger of extinction!"

"Just a minute. Slow down please… I have to take stock of what is being conveyed to me."

The information about the humans seemed to overwhelm Kerisay, as he took a step back and began to twitch nervously.

"Please ask Kerisay and don't feel shy. I am not trying to worry or trick you! We are friends, aren't we?"

"First, how has my mother communicated?" replied Kerisay in a tone that was a little tetchy and suggested that he felt that his mother should have told him more. This is what he found particularly disappointing.

"This sounds strange Kerisay, but she sent me a kind of telepathic message. I am telling you the truth. Hand on heart."

Kerisay now stood still, motionless, with his mouth agape. Whilst this conversation took place, Kerisay's father too was utterly dumbfounded to conclusively absorb the extraordinary information, being conveyed by his son's best friend.

"Believe me, I am not trying to be funny Zerisoyah. I am sorry to ask. Why would she send you... this message?" was the quizzical reply.

"I am truly unsure! Your mother was standing outside your front door, two days ago and it was 5.45 pm. In fact, I was on my way home from the local shops and noticed her seated on the porch steps of your home; she was looking completely exhausted. I asked her if I could assist and get her some water and even suggested that I should call my aunt, but she was adamant that she needed neither water nor assistance from my aunt. She emphasised her feelings with a resoundingly assertive no!

"Then paradoxically, she humbly wondered about my health and if I was hungry."

Kerisay was listening attentively.

"Moving surprisingly swiftly, in an almost magical manner, she went back inside and brought out a beautiful bowl of the most sumptuously delicious looking and freshest fruit imaginable. Your mother was very kind and courteous. I was overwhelmed with her generosity."

Kerisay turned to his father, whereupon the father raised his eyes, as a sign of complete surprise.

Then, in turn the father nonchalantly shrugged his shoulders in a manner to suggest uncertainty, as to where the conversation was leading.

"When she handed me the fruit bowl, I thanked her and before I headed home, she asked me to eat the large and fleshy berry-type fruit. As I began eating the fruit, I began to momentarily drift off to sleep, and then I felt as if your mother was talking to me in a different telepathic language."

"Telepathy — NO WAY!" exclaimed the father and son in unison.

"Yes, I am telling you the absolute truth," attested Zerisoyah.

"But I am unclear. There was not anything else?" retorted Kerisay.

"Listen Kerisay, whatever you know, I know. She also mentioned that there would be key information in the library and you could reach her via the first-floor landing mirror!"

"Why did you not tell me this immediately Zerisoyah?"

"I was scared. There was news spreading locally about your mother's disappearance and there were wider and scarier rumours that the C-Echelons were showing interest about your mother's whereabouts!"

"I have to go Zerisoyah. I am sorry," blurted Kerisay.

Zerisoyah looked a little surprised and sensed that her friend was not entirely satisfied, with the information she had imparted. She was torn, because the messages being received from Rolanda-Runa were not always complete. She felt there was a wilful impediment in the message transmission and that a negative energy form was trying to decrypt the information and then corrupt it.

Only entire and pure messages could completely make sense and incomplete or tampered information, could conceivably complicate matters, especially for sensitive souls.

Before she departed, she held out her outstretched hand in a sign of friendship and Kerisay shook her hand firmly, as a sign of trust.

At that precise moment, the message that Zerisoyah had received from Rolanda-Runa was relayed to Kerisay. Interestingly, Kerisay, who had his mind naturally elsewhere, did not immediately react.

The father turned to Zerisoyah and with a genuine apology exuded, "Please forgive us. We do believe you, but we don't have a moment to lose."

Zerisoyah nodded respectfully, as she realised the father's sincere sentiments and appreciated them. She recognised that they were in a hurry.

"Don't worry, I completely understand. If you need anything, please ask. You may find a silver box useful."

"Goodbye… Zerisoyah, a silver box?" Kerisay Senior replied in surprise and laden with emotion. He gently closed the front door.

Once Zerisoyah had departed, the father and son looked upstairs and then at each other. In synchronicity, they turned around 90 degrees and gazed with bated breath, in the direction of the stairs.

Fascinatingly, as Kerisay began to ascend the stairs, his friend's transmitted message was automatically being stored.

The information about a box had now been magically and automatically placed in one corner of Kerisay's brain. The young capybara's eyes blinked to subconsciously acknowledge what had been acknowledged.

As an additional thought, the father and son climbed the staircase in a galloping motion, the father leading the way. When they reached the landing on the first-floor, they immediately noticed the imposing nature of the heavy-looking magical mirror on the right-hand side. Previously, it was overlooked. Be that as it may, they turned a sharp left and headed towards the library, which oppositely faced the mirror and was situated three metres away from the top of the stairs.

Opening the library door, the father queried, "My son, it feels a little cold in here. Don't you think?"

"Too much! Yet, I can see some large metal boxes stacked on a burly and imposing table ahead of us. I did not realise how much space the table takes."

They walked briskly towards the metal boxes. Each box was silver in colour and was a perfect cube with a length, height, and width all measuring exactly 30 centimetres.

The boxes were positioned in rows, with four at the bottom, three on the next row up, two on the penultimate row, and one at the top. Ten boxes in total.

"I have no idea what your dear grandmother kept in these boxes. They are awfully heavy. Even, your mother prevented me from going anywhere near them!"

Kerisay's muscles around his eyes moved, as if he were raising his eyebrows.

"Anyway father, there is one box which is dated and can be seen. It is at the top of the pile of boxes. Can you see? It is the 10th box!"

"Oh, that one! That is... so interesting. Looks like the boxes are stacked like a towering pyramid?"

"The shape of the boxes is most engrossing," replied the son enthusiastically.

"My son, once we have the box, let's find out if we can unlock it?"

The father reached up and immediately grabbed the 10th metal box they had in focus. On closer inspection, the date and time read, "11th May at 5.45 pm. The year 2163. Dream absorbed successfully and completely."

"The box requires a key to open it, father. But... look at the date! It is the same... day as when... Zerisoyah saw mother!"

"This is most interesting. Was there anything in the messages you received from your mother that could help us unlock this box?"

"I need to think father... please, may I have a moment. Actually, she did leave me her favourite family picture with a poem in my bedside drawer. She knew I misplaced objects, but hoped I could at least read the poem, which I never got around to doing. It is worth looking at now, because I have no idea how this box can be conventionally unlocked."

"Good thinking! Can you find this poem my son?"

The son departed without a word and ran hurriedly towards his bedroom, which was equidistant between the first-floor magic mirror and the library. He darted around the corner of his slightly ajar bedroom door like a figure dancer and scootered towards the bedside table, where his heart sunk a little. The three-drawer unit was cluttered with countless layers of items, including an assortment of bibs and bobs, plus newspaper cuttings, though the medals from his school's summer sports day event, on the 13th of July 2162, momentarily lifted his spirits.

The young capybara reverentially dropped his head and closed his determined eyes tightly, uttering the following words silently, in order to focus his mind on the picture search.

Heavenly and loving spirit
That guides our world.
Hear my prayer and don't demerit.
I have tried to act honourably
Be humble and earn merits.

Where there is hope,
Bring me inspiration.
Let me search not in vain, or fail to cope,
Instead persevere, find the picture poem
That appears on a written envelope.

He plunged his hands into the assorted pile, but there was nothing.

Reciting the silent prayer once more that his mother had transmitted for lost items, he single-mindedly plunged his hands deeper into the depths of the three-drawer table and was able to miraculously detect the smoothness of a picture that lifted his soul.

He gently peeled the picture away from the attached torn and slightly sticky, white, frail and opened envelope. This was the treasured and uplifting picture he was desperately seeking, depicting a wonderful family holiday!

At once, he flipped the picture of his mother over and on the reverse, saw the handwriting he recognised and in a euphoric voice, volubly exclaimed, "It's mother's poem!"

His father could hear his son and placed the metal box carefully on the wooden floor, in a gesture of respect, whereupon he rushed along the corridor and directly into his son's room.

"My son, my son, what have you found?"

"I have scrutinised the item. On the reverse of the picture is something interesting… to activate the silver box and a mirror."

"Go ahead and read that out," retorted the father, which the son undertook hurriedly, which caused two key words to be left out.

Magic [silver] box, a perfect cube.
Reveal your secrets, we plead, are true.
Help us deftly, whilst we muse.
Guide us [now], so we are not confused!

"Nothing's happened. Slowly and clearly peruse once more Kerisay. Remember to add the words 'silver' and 'now' in the first and last lines respectively!"

The son proceeded to follow his father's instructions and recited the poem, with due diligence.

This time, he emphasised the words he had omitted.

There was an apprehensive pause... and they looked at each other intently, trying to ascertain whether there would be any reaction to what had been read.

In the library, they could tantalisingly hear a tinkling sound and then more a grating noise, which became clearer, as the volume increased automatically: a metal object clattering around the four legs of the table. The reciting of the enchantment was the catalyst!

"Wait father, there is a further message. It is concerning the mirror and I assume this will be spoken with deliberation."

"Don't read that as yet. I sense we may have to take one step at a time my son."

They spun around on their heels and raced back into the library. On the floor, the metal box the father had placed on the ground had its lid thrust open and its contents had been spilled onto the floor. The inside of the box was cold to touch.

In front of them, they could see a small, delicate, and a quite beautiful square piece of magical cloth.

Strangely delicate to touch and on closer inspection, a surprisingly pristine looking white linen, with a width and height of 30 centimetres; it proceeded to fold itself in half, producing the appearance of an isosceles triangle and was resting peacefully within a transparent plastic A3 sized sleeve.

It was ensconced amongst an extraordinary collection of different coloured pens, pencils, erasers, and rulers, all in groups of three.

Rolanda-Runa had a penchant for hoarding items and the number 3 was her favourite number. The collection of this stationery was motivated by her love of writing stories, which was a leisurely pursuit she adored the most.

Strangely, two identical, white, 5-centimetre-sized square cards emblazoned with the words "Wait" and "Stop" could be seen underneath the linen.

These were two words that Rolanda-Runa did not particularly like hearing or using and chastised her husband and son, if these words were ubiquitously uttered.

On the front of the first card, beneath the word "Wait", it clearly stated the following.

CLOSELY OBSERVE THE MAGIC LINEN — THIS IS CRUCIAL TO YOUR QUEST! BE CALM AND PATIENT. THESE ARE VIRTUES.

Whereas on the second card, underneath the "Stop" word, the enchantment pertaining to the Magic 1st Floor Landing Mirror was presented in full for the first time. Interestingly, on the reverse of this specific card, was an added note. Regrettably, being unfortunately impatient and hasty, the capybaras failed to inspect it.

It read the following, "Beware of a dishonest hatch that tries to vivaciously illuminate the number 3, which can make your journey at any point more challenging. The one you actually want will be numbered 3, but look simple in comparison, plus possess my initials RR, positioned in the bottom left-hand corner. You will notice the appropriate one, as it will appear near or under your feet and emit a warm glow. The remaining hatches will be nervous or can be dangerous. I have divulged this belatedly because I almost forgot! Sorry. PS – If you use the wrong hatch, you may have difficulty getting back or worse! Be careful please."

One may assume, the young capybara briefly felt the imprint texture of the words on the second card, yet the presence and magical appeal of the linen cloth appeared to place other considerations on the back burner. Moreover, and incredibly, none of the fabric's edges were torn, or looked frail.

The father carefully removed the linen and as he did so, the material seemed to be activated and come to life, frantically moving around, as if it had its sleep disturbed, and then it seemed to regain a sense of sublime composure. Little by little, energy began flooding back and its molecules hungrily absorbed even the faintest rays of sunlight.

It then comfortably leaped up into the air, with the grace of a ballet dancer, whereupon it swirled and flipped around like a seasoned acrobat and stayed up in the air for at least 30 seconds.

The magical material confidently appeared to be surveying its immediate surroundings.

Extraordinarily, it transformed its demeanour and appearance and swooped down like a deadly bird of prey (reminiscent of folk tales about the Giant-Flying-Prey-Master), and then the fabric magically swayed, metamorphized forthwith to look like an innocent new-born capybara. In its new form, it glided to and fro in the air like a cherub, before remarkably descending into the son's right-hand, who bemused had inadvertently stood back, a few seconds earlier aghast with his hands in the air.

The father and son looked at each other in complete astonishment.

At eye level, the son sensed that the piece of linen, was at peace and he gently cradled the square piece of linen, which then once more altered and appeared to warm reassuringly, as if it were trying to communicate compassionately.

Astonishingly, it was like the warmth that Kerisay's mother emitted, whenever she was in one's presence.

Now, it impressively switched from a white hue to a slightly darker, crimson colour and began to reveal little by little, information in the form of text and images, in a delicately forthright and white font style, as to where his mother was located.

The typical salutation was undoubtedly Rolanda-Runa's.

The father and son looked on without a word, completely frozen to the spot, as each word and image magically appeared, before their disbelieving eyes. The use of a plural, first person possessive pronoun, caught them off guard.

"We need to read and study carefully what is being revealed. This will be crucial to our efforts in finding her," reasonably speculated the father.

There were identifiable and striking anomalies in this magical information — contrasting markedly with the relative detail Kerisay provided that was more meaningful and coherent.

The young son bemusedly nodded. The images however, undoubtedly required a level of interpretation.

Penultimately, as if to soothe any doubting mind, the images began to be labelled. The room glowed in synchronicity with an incandescent intensity, reminding the capybaras of this fact, so that they could try to make slightly more sense of where Rolonda-Runa was.

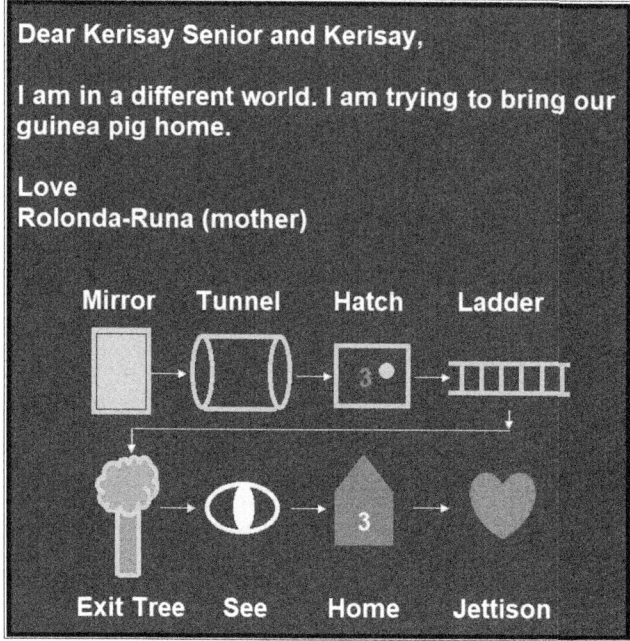

The extraordinary magic was spellbinding to observe. As a consequence, they stood rooted and unabashed to the spot, finding it difficult to speak. There were unanswered questions that filled the air and in every corner of the room. Likewise, they were distinctly not sure what adventure would befall them, but one innate matter was without dispute — they were keen to find Rolanda-Runa and time was of the essence.

Then finally, albeit in a manner that appeared slightly hurried, initial information began to fade, revealing new clues. Later, these clues would vanish into the ether.

> **Walk through the mirror precisely at 18:00 and no earlier or later. This is important.**
>
> **You will enter a tunnel and after you depart the tunnel, there will be hatches above you. Choose the one numbered 3. A ladder will drop down.**
>
> **The ladder will carry you forward. Hold on very tight as it may speed up.**
>
> **Next, it will appear that you are inside a large oak tree and from there you will see a world. This world is not ours. Exit the tree and there in front of you a house like ours will be clearly in view.**
>
> **You will feel strange at first, but light-footed and able to walk through rooms. Anyhow, I will be there to greet you and you will hear the pulse of my heartbeat.**

Chapter 9 – Entrance to the Other World

"Father, what's the time?"

"Kerisay, it is approaching 18:00. Are you thinking what I am thinking?"

"Yes, the mirror will open soon, as a matter of course."

"Precisely. It only felt like mid-afternoon earlier, but how time is flying? At any rate, we have to proceed most cautiously."

The father and son faced each other and were frightfully uncertain of what to expect from the mirror.

Then suddenly, they heard a little light crackle, followed by a shimmering light trickle out from the edges of the mirror. This was now proceeded by further brilliant, but gradual and tiny bursts of light, followed by greater intermittent crackles, each increasing with a miniscule amount of intensity.

This continued unabated.

Almost immediately, the mirror began to transfigure and the colours of the rainbow could be seen. Multiple rainbows appeared and at the bottom of each rainbow, flashing images of Rolanda-Runa could be seen. It was as if she was reminding her family of her presence in the other world.

"My son, do you have the special enchanted message concerning the mirror?"

"Yes, I shall read it out."

"Remember, try to not feel agitated. What happens next is crucial."

"Okay, I understand… I shall try."

The son vocalised slowly and deliberately. His voice was understandably tempered with emotion, but he soon realised the importance of remaining calm and composed.

Determination filled every countenance of his face, whereupon he gritted his teeth and then began to utter the following instantly.

Magic 1st Floor Landing Mirror,
That will start to shimmer.
Please show us where our beloved one is,
We are no behemoths, we wish to live in bliss.
Help us to find, be safe and bring home,
Without delay, be focused and not aimlessly roam.
We respect your infinite power,
And we'll heed warnings, be virtuous, not devour.

At that instant, the middle of the mirror seemed to push its sides open and fold inwards, almost in the manner of a concertina and as its structure moved, a bedazzling and gaping hole appeared. In the distance, they could see a tunnel like cylinder and further on lights flickering.

They could eerily hear Rolanda-Runa's fading voice calling out repeatedly and pleadingly, "Hurry, please hurry."

Both father and son moved forward with trepidation. The father entered the mirror first and was followed step by step, by his son. All round there was silence and they nervously proceeded. The roof of the cylinder undulated, so they had to force themselves to crouch down uncomfortably. In fact, at times they had to crawl and after moving for two minutes, which was agonising for them, the light at the end was larger and emitted a warm and reassuring glow.

Their hearts were momentarily lifted.

The father exited the cylinder first, his son was not far behind. The father now turned around and could see their mirror in the distant. As he adjusted his straining eyes and refocused, the entrance of the cylinder seemed strangely further away — more than was imaginable.

"That is extraordinary… amazing," quivered Kerisay.

At that very moment, there was something stirring in the vicinity, which unnerved them both. A blanket of fog suddenly descended from out of the blue, yet they purposefully marched on. Any sign of weakness or hesitation would not lift the fog. Proceeding bravely, the father then took a large gulp of air and wondered if what he had done was right. Namely have his son accompany him.

It is noteworthy that on reflection, crucial detail had been lacking from the son's received messages, which would be alluded to on the following pages.

Be that as it may, at this juncture, the father and son were in a marvellous, highly decorated and spacious room, an environment that was staggeringly beautiful.

The room was splattered with pictures of austere looking capybaras, waving magical wands and wearing an attire that appeared to be from a time period that was understandably unrecognisable. This room was enchantingly lit, but naturally there were no windows, just some wax candles, burning incandescently, twelve feet or more above the capybaras and these candle lanterns were hanging elegantly from a ceiling that at its centre tapered off into infinite darkness and looked for the world, from their angle, like an upside cone of sorts.

Located to the capybaras' left and right, in all the empty spaces, above and below their feet also, were wooded hatches. Slowly, but undeniably carefully, the animals moved on. However, they were too many hatches to count and too much noise was being generated.

Indeed, if an attempt was made to identify the total number of hatches before their eyes, the hatches would move around randomly, in order to deliberately disorientate, at a frightening speed.

Perfectly carved, many hatches were crimson in colour, with rounded silver door handles. The hatches under their feet, would tantalisingly flip up a corner of its door, when approached, in order to entice their opening, or would hoover up to them and rotate in order to encourage further curiosity and greater observation.

Besides, a few hatches had surprisingly tiny dark and foreboding patterns on the front of the hatch, sneakily concealed in the corners, which were unnoticeable (and not relayed by Rolanda-Runa), until one got very close, whilst one hatch looked just plain, yet was attempting to gently slip its way forward undetected.

The other crimson coloured hatches possessed an exuding eeriness that were terribly unnatural, plus a peculiar heat that was decidedly unfriendly and would pierce certain parts of the animals' feet.

The hatch, initially and nervously sneaked judiciously forward; in fact, looked rather ordinary. It emitted a gentle heat and approached them respectfully, producing a wonderful comforting warmth that in contrast, was interestingly heart-warming, when compared to the other more belligerent hatches.

What is more, the gentle hatch looked rather charmingly unusual, as the character on its front looked like the letter E, but was overturned and situated horizontally.

However, the capybaras seeing hundreds of rapidly moving hatches, were feeling considerably overwhelmed. In addition, to add to their woes, a number of the hatches were confusingly similar in size, but of course, wide enough for a capybara to fit and the hatches had silver characters (some of which were a strange metallic shade).

Another hatch in the distance, which was deceitfully numbered 3, appeared to radiate brilliantly. It sensed that the capybaras had missed the simple hatch they should have focused on.

A light automatically shone up emblazoned with that number to attract their attention. Surprisingly, it did not move around like the others, but in a cunning manner, as if it were trying to entrap the capybaras.

As their animals' nervousness grew, they mistakenly moved forward towards the superciliously deceitful hatch, whilst the other wooden hatches on the floor, or to their sides and above their head moved haphazardly to mirror their walking speed. By then, the plain hatch had been shunted away.

Then, sensing the capybaras were possibly getting closer to the deceitful hatch, the other hatches in allegiance, appeared to start playing a mathematical cat and mouse game, moving quickly after every fifteen seconds and covering as much distance as they could, pausing for five seconds and then speeding round once more, in order to disorientate the animals and weaken their resolve.

This approach, began to slow down the forward movement of the capybaras to almost a standstill and cause them frustration.

After a while, they realised that they were being toyed with and collectively, with authority shouted, "WAIT!"

It was not premeditated, but the word was uttered in sheer tired exasperation.

Finally, the hatches stopped moving and the deceitful hatch appeared in front of their eyes and disbelievingly shunted the other hatches away and glided magically to move above the animals' heads.

They locked their eyes on the hatch and the hatch opened and a ladder instantly dropped down. At that precise moment, they turned to each other in perceived relief, but paradoxically, from their perspective, the ladder then sullenly pulled up and the hatch slammed tightly closed.

The capybaras were greatly irritated. Perhaps the instructions garnered were not entirely correct, they contended. They glared around, over their shoulders and above, in order to try and gain some further perspective of their surroundings.

Now, all the hatches begun moving around the sides and above their heads. All the while, these hatches were tightly locked.

When the movement paused, they saw that the deceitful one cunningly moved to their left, tempting them.

Through unmitigated will power, they kept their eyesight on the hatch, focused intensively, mentally urging the hatch to release the ladder. This was their mistake. A grave error induced, through tiredness and a lack of calm thinking.

Retaining a firm visual proximity on the hatch they approached the wooden frame in a concerted effort.

Together, they uttered the word detested by Rolanda-Runa but delivered resoundingly, "WAIT!"

This hatch paused. Tentatively, little by little, they carefully opened the deceitful hatch. It had rotated anti-clockwise and was strangely positioned diagonally, so naturally, the capybaras anticipated that they would be uncomfortably walking at an angle. This is not what they quite expected!

Interestingly, this deceitful hatch then commenced spinning 360 degrees; it was almost a tantalising action, as if they were being both teased and reminded to utilise this particular hatch.

Now, peering inside the hatch, which the father and son took turns in doing, made them feel rather a little queasy. It was dark as the darkest night inside this object, yet every thirteen seconds, they could see a faint flicker of light at the end of what really was a long tunnel; they were still rather apprehensive.

Suddenly, a new ladder started to magically take centre stage in front of their quite disbelieving eyes, as if to alleviate their intense sense of discomfort and it was no ordinary ladder.

To further mitigate their anxiousness, as the ladder object rolled out before them, it dramatically changed its angle of projection, to a precise forty-five degrees clockwise and seemed to automatically rotate the hatch in the process, so that the countenance of the hatch no longer looked like a rhombus, but a square.

As the ladder moved further out in the direction of the capybaras, what was distinctly noticeable was that it appeared to have an inordinate number of rungs on the ladder (especially if one tried to see its end point).

The rungs were smooth in texture and perfectly cylindrical in shape and connected to the rails seamlessly, so it was impossible to see how the pieces were fixed together. Indeed, there was no sign of imperfection on the ladder.

The father could only shake his head in sheer disbelief and marvel at the craft and ingenuity of the ladder builders.

"Whoever built this structure was incredible."

"I agree father."

"My son, I will go inside first."

"Father, are you sure?"

"Yes, don't worry. The light in the distance, will be my guide.

The elder capybara proceeded cautiously forward and low and behold, as he moved on, he could see the light in the distance getting just a little closer, with every inch by inch advance.

"Father, can I enter the tunnel now?" called out Kerisay.

"Yes. Be careful of the rungs on the ladder and follow me. Watch every step."

After ten minutes, the father paused for a breather. When he took stock of how far he had progressed, he could see ahead more lights. His son was in pursuit.

Subsequently, the father could discern faint noises, laughter, chattering, plus a scary, strange disturbance.

They proceeded further regardless, without any apparent and outwardly qualms.

"My son, how are you doing?"

"A little tired father, but I am determined."

"Great to hear. Any moment now and hopefully we should be in the other world," before he quipped, with a tender but humourous tone, "may be my dearest wife had been in a rush, because there's been a surprising dearth of facts. I did not realise how much exertion would be needed for this quest!"

Kerisay was fleetingly feeling more hopeful that he would see his mother and smiled at his father's attempt at humour.

The father now felt as if there was an impediment, which was peculiarly heavy – perhaps irritatingly borne out of weariness. After all, he had found sleeping, since his wife disappeared almost impossible and was looking worse for wear.

He struggled a little onward, leading the way and then reacquainted himself with what was slowing them down. In actuality, he thought his wife could hear him and wondered whether she made the process a little more strenuous, by omitting key information in their adventure.

There was an inordinate amount of plant life around him, so shoving this material asunder, which was now popping up, felt empowering and surprisingly reinvigorating.

"Kerisay, these plants are a nuisance. How are you doing?"

"This is tough going father. Could you help?"

The father turned around and could see long, green, shrub leaves enveloping his son and impeding progress.

"How quickly have they reappeared?" the father acknowledged, before continuing, "let me pull these leaves away… is that better?"

"Yes, father it's somewhat better. Thank you."

"Oh no. There are… still more annoying leaves in front of us," adumbrated the senior capybara.

The father gritted his teeth and tugged away, grasping bunches of the leaves in irritation.

Then, with one almighty heave, which was difficult in the circumstances, as the space was particularly tight, he confoundedly ripped away those leaves interrupting his view, with unforeseen gusto.

He heaved an almighty sigh of relief.

At this juncture, the father and son were now trying desperately to gaze out into the new world. In one sense, they were slightly distracted and forgot about the primary goal. In lieu, their charming faces huddled together could see a completely different place, which was startlingly strange, incredibly absorbing, plus a rather awe-inspiring environment.

Unsurprisingly, they had never observed creatures like this, wearing multi-coloured clothes, stylish footwear, a variety of extraordinary hats and driving strange vehicles. There was a cacophony of colourful noises.

Individuals from this strange world, were seen listening seriously to music, whilst nodding and singing to the right of the capybaras. Another group, positioned north-west and perhaps ten metres from the view of the father and son, were sitting casually on a bench, adjacent to a busy road, running in parallel.

A vehicle that had paused on the same road nearby, was emitting loud melodic music that was soothingly alluring at a distance, powerful, uplifting and immeasurably refreshing, but then, another vehicle rushed past the stationary one, with a whoosh and their music was such a contrast; it was unquestionably blaring, harsh, discernibly discordant and the words being emitted from the song were completely indecipherable.

The capybaras shook their heads to clear the latter sound.

Then, Kerisay Senior trying not to be seen, first gently pushed his left shoulder and forelimb through the exit of the magic tree. He attempted to delicately pick at the strands of grass. What bewildered him was that his hand seemed to move through the grass, as if the grass did not exist – or more pertinently his hand, in any tangible form.

As he intensively studied his hands and limbs, they remarkably began to speedily disappear the more he moved further into the new world.

When he took a backward movement, he could see the contours of his body clearly, but any forward motion, meant his limbs were becoming vaguer.

This alarmed him, but he could not turn back now. However, when he turned and gazed at his son, who was in a trance at what he was observing, he could actually see him.

"Wait... wait there please, my son," he conveyed assertively, but in a pensive and considerate tone, with just a hint of worry. The father did not like to show any signs of weakness to his son.

Kerisay Senior closed his eyes and proceeded. He had come this far. There was no turning back!

As he left the relative security of the tree and stood on the soft grass, he stared out into this new world. Yet, he noticed that there were weighted footprints that had broken the long, tender grass, leaving an indelible like impression.

Whilst he was doing this, his son's eyes were growing wider and his mouth opened in sheer amazement.

"My son, let me look around. Don't come out as yet... I need to check!"

Kerisay's demeanour was dramatically transformed, prompting a truly flustered reply, "Be safe please… — yes, yes and I will wait here, inside the tree."

Chapter 10 – An Encounter to Remember

Meanwhile, back in the capybara world, the dark energy force SSK1, had already begun recalibrating and thinking how it could cause discomfort to its nemesis.

The quiet "retreat" by SSK1 was a strategic one and it found cruel comfort in penetrating the weak and selfish minds of the C-Echelons to extract information about the capybara community.

The C-Echelons were easily bribed through the promise of untold riches and wealth. Slowly, but surely, they were induced to gradually reveal, who they thought was the last descendent from the wizard family: the amazing Rolanda-Runa. The evil energy form was able to calibrate that information and finally deduce that the special capybara had a link to its past. That undeniable connection meant a foe.

SSK1 was intent to send out a combination of conflicting, cluttering, confoundingly indecipherable messages to Rolanda-Runa and to her immediate family members: Kerisay Senior and young Kerisay.

The wicked creature was testing the water, so to speak. SSK1 wanted to cause pain to those Rolanda-Runa loved most and sow the seeds of maximum confusion.

Of the three capybaras, it adroitly sensed that Kerisay Senior was the one whom could be manipulated the most, followed by the son. SSK1's honed curse was immediate.

To those, who impede my progress,
Let them know, I will never show forgiveness.
To those, who disrupt my advances.
Let their mind suffer with anxiety and painful chances.

Fool, Kerisay Senior, believe you'll find your wife;
A cloud will envelope and confusion rife.
Begin to see not what you believe — be glib.
Prevail you not, sow doubts when you adlib.

You will see, what I want you to see,
From the position of the Java kapok tree.
Northerly, there will be a blurry vision
And you won't be mindful of this disposition.

Kerisay Senior and your offspring too,
Shall be bemused and have no clue.
The mighty Java kapok trees,
Neither a saviour, nor the bee's knees.

You'll tempt fate and,
Be separated, damned, canned,
So, you'll think what's is real,
Your thoughts I shall steal.

Whenever you meet a tricky challenge, whinge.
You will be confused and verily cringe.
Rushed, there'll be a mistaken ruse.
Each family member alone, minds never fused.

Simply oblivious to any curse, Kerisay Senior still intrinsically moved with extreme caution.

He was undeterred in one sense, as his primary goal was finding his beloved wife. The instructions on the linen cloth were useful, but excruciatingly baffling, he contemplated.

At that exact moment, he felt something strange enter his mind.

It caused him to feel unsteady on his feet and he shook his head repeatedly, like an individual who was disbelieving or trying to eradicate an annoying sound.

Nonetheless, after fully exiting the tree, he thought he could see the contours of the specified and destined northerly house, but at a stroke, a curtain of dense and impenetrable fog descended over his eyes.

Forthwith, as he peered farther ahead, he could see no house, but an interminable field of uncut grass!

"Had he and his son walked through the correct hatch?" he asked himself out loud.

Looking around, invisible to the world around him, he began to think deeply. Seconds passed.

Then the proverbial penny dropped!

Panic was etched all over the contours of his face. He began to move nervously and contemplated how he could leave this world, without being noticed.

He obviously knew, how to get back to the tree, but he was equivocal, as to whether he could be hindered in this world and more pertinently, he was stricken with worry that he was in the wrong time period.

His mind's view was growing cloudier and this promoted intrinsic methodical head scratching, displaying a grave moment of uncertainty. As he turned, with his head from one side to another, he could still admiringly glance the tree he had exited.

Plus, the footprints on the nearby luscious grass softened the movement of his feet, generating a strange comfort. Yet peering ahead in a northerly direction, brought grave hesitation to his mind.

There was a sense of bitter sweetness too. Yes, there was a predicament he faced that required urgent attention. Despite this incontrovertible fact, he was in the midst of a world that possessed so many beautiful contradictions.

On one hand, the clouds were high up in the sky, the sun shone radiantly, the ambience appeared energetic, plus the capybara could sense here in this specific area, a camaraderie between the creatures.

Within a few moments, he could quickly reflect on his location. He retrospectively noticed that within this particular setting, the humans walked upright and there was an apparent purpose, in how they conducted themselves.

There was the occasional act of courtesy shown and a couple of elderly inhabitants of this world, were assisted to cross strange looking roads, with what appeared to be a kind helper.

Over and above, Kerisay Senior discerned that the massive advertising pictures were everywhere; they were projecting vibrant and contented individuals, within a convivial surrounding.

This perception differed markedly from what had been relayed to him earlier, about humans.

Near another park bench, further behind the Java kapok tree, whilst he was hazily moving, a colourful headline with an image featuring one human, smiling to an implied group of acquaintances, who were all attentively listening — with a combination of fascinated, yet concerned countenances.

"CAN HUMANS BE TRUSTED TO SAVE THE ENVIRONMENT?"

Then underneath, he saw a subtitle, which rather ominously presented a stark warning message.

"Leading international scientist believes that current conflicts are so volatile and dangerous that they will irretrievably damage the environment and lead to our demise. We must, as humans, treat other creatures and our planet Earth with respect or else! There must be more peaceful protests."

Other bright and blissfully appealing images nearby were promoting food, sports, language specialists and holidays, juxtaposed with wonderful pictures of individuals respectively enjoying a sumptuous meal and the sunshine.

The reference to language specialists was most intriguing, as the father vividly remembered seeing a plain looking hatch with a character on its front, appearing to show a letter from the Cyrillic alphabet.

This recollection caused a moment of disquiet!

For all that, everywhere within the immediate proximity, he could also witness pockets of endearing human interaction, where individuals were in joyful and animated conversations.

"Humans? These individuals must be sentient! My goodness, I have never seen a civilisation like this before," Kerisay Senior mulled quietly to himself.

In the distance, he could hear the faint voice of his perturbed son. The emanating tone sounded more and more desperate and reality driven.

"Father, father… what is going on? What is going on? Why are you unfocused? Hurry."

Kerisay Senior snapped out of his own "realm".

For a while at least, he was carried away with the excitement of being in a new world. Everyone in this strange microcosm appeared so far as kind and sensible, the father naively and dreamily believed. How wrong could he be?

Intriguingly and all the same, his footprints were leaving a growing gathering of puzzled looks and calls from other humans to investigate these patterns and its direction.

As he moved hither and thither, his footsteps were appearing rapidly, before the disbelieving eyes of the humans, more and more of whom were congregating from the purposes of impending action: pointing, gesticulating, hypothesising, pondering and planning.

It was taking place in real-time and as the number of patterns (from the bird's eye view) increased and crisscrossed, the humans began to become nervous and fearful of the unknown.

There was an added sense of irritation and rage in one or two of the humans, as they were of the opinion that this was a sign of the end of the world, which contrasted sharply with the earlier happier and smiling advertising images.

When the complacent father belatedly recognised their unhealthy interest, his apprehension grew exponentially, contrasting markedly from the glossy advertisements: promoting harmony, collaboration and coexistence.

He turned around sharply and proceeded to gallop towards the tree. Now, looking at the tree, focusing on its size surprised him, as he was doubting whether he could squeeze back in. There were doubts clouding his mind.

The inside of the tree was quite an extraordinary chamber and it accommodated any size. In fact, the Java kapok, magically accommodated capybaras, but to re-enter the tree, was a different kettle of fish and moreover, a matter that incredulously the father had not thoroughly or properly considered.

"Which limb would be used first to enter the tree?" he cried out in consternation.

Confusion was reigning and the curse was having an impact on this thinking.

Retrospectively on exiting the tree and at that precise juncture, he prematurely expected to see his wife at once, who in turn would have the knowledge and skill, to re-enter the tree.

But the environment was confusingly apparent — to him, it appeared that he was arguably not in the same time zone as his wife. Or perhaps in a parallel dimension? He could not be certain one way or another.

He began calling out to his son in a hushed voice at first, in an attempt to not be heard, but then more volubly that was now full of panic and tension.

The humans could hear sounds of a language, which was distinctly unrecognisable on Earth and it was a bizarre communication form they alarmingly absorbed.

In earshot of the father, one human, who had designated himself as a leader, commenced to illogically holler, "CALL THE POLICE! ALIENS! Find and catch the invaders."

This triggered pandemonium amongst the humans, who began to show impatience and anger.

"Go back and get help from Zerisoyah and her sister. Go now, please! I am being pursued and tracked by the humans!"

His son's demeanour naturally transformed. He looked absolutely horrified.

"Pursued... and tracked?" the son squealed.

"Yes, flee Kerisay... now. I can see a river about 100 metres away and will stay there and hide. Go my son, go, GO".

This was the first time the son had heard his father raise his voice to the rafters and appear immensely agitated.

Kerisay was frozen to the spot.

Suddenly, he could hear his mother's soporific voice, "Do not be afraid Kerisay, I am here in this world, there is a spell that has been cast over your father, so his view is clouded."

The surprising tone of the voice combined a sense of measured urgency, but underpinned with cool collectedness, whereupon it became beseeching.

"Find Zerisoyah. Find her! If you leave the safety of this tree and follow your father, you could end up in real danger."

"Why could I not have heard her voice before?" he contemplated.

The mother's voice again re-entered his mind and elucidated, "I was not sure, how far you were into your journey, but when I heard the human commotion and noticed the tree, I could see your father. He can't see me. The humans won't stop pursuing him. The situation is perilous."

Kerisay felt a jolt to his body.

His mother's voice continued, "Humans can be wonderful, but there had been occasions in their own troubled history, when they reacted fearfully to the unknown and without thinking, they tragically forgot their humanity and wars were savagely fought. Terrible, terrible, TERRIBLE events. Now go please my son! Depart, before it's too late."

The young capybara shook his head in both a sign of dread and bewilderment.

However, he trusted the voice and as he simultaneously and dangerously peeped out of the tree (creepily, his vision seemed momentarily askew), he sensed that his galloping father had frantically whizzed farther from the safety of the tree.

The young capybara felt helpless. Ahead, he could vaguely see the creatures agitating. They looked in his direction and pointed collectively.

The young capybara was filled with fear from head to toe. He turned swiftly on his heels and rushed back through the cylinder and in the direction of the room of hatches.

As he proceeded, the trek was not a matter he was enjoying at all. He was overcome with heightened fear.

The tunnel appeared unusually dark and foreboding.

Though, from the perspective of distance, initially together with his father, the tunnel did not at that time, seem quite as interminable.

Now, the return journey did give the impression of being an endless trudge and the tunnel was apparently deceptively longer. His footsteps staggered a little from acute exhaustion.

Then, the capybara began to spontaneously utter a mantra quietly to himself, which he found surprising, "Calm... down, calm down, be composed, don't... rush... don't rush," repeating these a further three times.

The repetition of the innate words spoken serenely, whilst closing his eyes in meditation, generated a more relaxed ambience and this synchronised with the appearance of a light at the end of the tunnel.

He thus figured that if he could perceptibly keep his eyes closed longer and recite the mantra, this perhaps would in turn, surely allow his tendency to have frayed nerves, to be lessened little by little.

Ergo, a calmer disposition would naturally develop.

An unruffled approach could be pursued and allow him to focus, think clearly and with precision, as well as draw nearer to the exit of the tunnel.

He further gathered his thoughts and began to rhythmically reassure himself through the mantra.

The heartbeat at the start of the return journey had earlier been racing, but the new composure facilitated the subduing of his fear (not the conquering), albeit temporarily.

Now, in front of him was the tunnel exit, which naturally had a solid wooden door hatch blocking his way and uncompromisingly uncooperative to boot (slyly so).

Yearnfully, he pushed his left shoulder against the door, but it seemed rather recalcitrant and caused an unfriendly rebound, forcibly pushing back the capybara, as if it were saying that respect needed to be shown.

Kerisay, being a capybara with nous, considered an alternative approach. Perhaps, if he spoke soothingly and kindly to the door and not in a hurried manner, the door may be more amenable.

"Hatch door that bars my exit, do open?"

The deceiving hatch was not in a mood to free the capybara.

"Object that bars my exit, kindly allow me to leave?"

Still there was no approving response.

"Perhaps, if I make reference to my mother's name?" the young capybara hypothesised in a clear manner to himself.

"Dear object that bars my exit, kindly open, so I can assist Rolanda-Runa?"

A few moments elapsed and then the exit door opened tantalisingly and then shut even firmer, with a hollow sound, resonating around the young capybara's ears.

Kerisay shook his head to clear the sound.

Again, Kerisay repeated the request, in a pleading manner, albeit using slightly different words. The request was expressed also with gentleness and reverence.

"Hatch door, I beseech you. Humbly I ask for your intercession. Please allow me a safe passage? I wish to assist my mother Rolanda-Runa."

There was silence and a feeling of resignation.

Then, to his complete astonishment the hatch door began to first creak, then groan and finally an opening to allow the capybara was permitted, whereupon, the door chortled sarcastically.

The capybara was palpably unimpressed and as he walked through, he brushed forcibly against the door, whilst exiting, wherefore causing its hinges to jolt.

The door appeared to react meekly, as if it had been chastised. In addition, the door handled that had glowed vibrantly, as it opened, finally accepted the request after the third attempt of asking. It had not realised that its disrespectful and churlish attitude, would cause the capybara's angry response. It had sensed the desperation in the capybara and wanted to exact a cruel price.

Now for the time being, the hatch door had humbly acknowledged its "misdemeanour" and the colour of its handle began to gradually lose its radiant and brash shine. Instead, the handle appeared to take on the appearance of a dull hue, to reflect its bruised feelings.

However, this reactionary and surly door would soon revert to type.

Chapter 11 – The Room of Hatches

The capybara gazed measuredly at his surroundings. He took a gulp and was completely in awe at the Room of Hatches!

His father had led the way previously, but this time he was on his own and this made he feel distinctly uncomfortable.

Naturally, there would be a need to navigate around the hatches. These hatch objects were not apparently inanimate. Many of them exuded pernicious behaviour and moved accordingly. When the young capybara moved left, they would move right, whilst if he moved forward, they moved forward.

At least, when his father was there, they could work together — now, he was alone.

Somehow, Kerisay plucked up every ounce of additional courage and decided that enough was enough. He wanted to take control and show his parents that he could with be courageous, reliable and trustworthy. That he could cope with this adventure.

The capybara moved forward cautiously.

Nonetheless, this slight movement trigged a concerted response from the hatches all round him and they moved in unison, like a gang, with great rapacious rapidity. The purpose was to frighten, confuse and ultimately prevent Kerisay from leaving, which at this point was successful.

The capybara's perceived nervousness took its toll and the young animal's mind starting behaving oddly, impacting his mental alertness and causing his fatigued legs to droop, his eyes to close, his head to drop, giving way to pervasive silence. It was quiet everywhere!

Serendipitously, the hatches would react to sound. What occurred next, would be just a figment of his vivid imagination.

Surprisingly and against the grain, the now dreaming capybara identified that one hatch began to move cautiously towards him. It had slipped through the melee and gone unnoticed by the other hatches. The warmth being emitted from the hatch was noticeable, prompting Kerisay to gently assume he was placing his front leg forward. The heat was placating and reassuring, causing his slumbering eyes to be at peace.

"Was this the hatch that should be opened?" the capybara contemplated mistily.

His conjecture saw the gentle hatch responding positively and slowly, whilst the light being emitted from within grew, as if it were encouraging the capybara to open it. The light was pleasant in appearance and soothing. However, the young capybara was reticent for obvious reasons, especially as on route to the human world, he and his father had in error selected a dubiously duplicitous hatch.

Obviously, a hatch of this nature could cunningly decide at a whim, how comfortable or difficult your journey to and from the destination should be.

All the while, the collection of other hatches appeared concerned by the actions of the gentle hatch and began moving indignantly around and brutally pressuring the gentle one, through aggressive movements and making harsh noises.

But this anomalous and kind hatch, was not for deviating and what is more, the reference to the nature of this hatch was not a misnomer.

The sensitively warm rays of light were increasingly undulating in potency.

Indeed, flattery or no flattery, would prevent it from rebelling and encouraging the capybara from opening its hatch door.

At this thought, the other hatches changed tact. They proceeded to move with greater speed and surprising dexterity.

Their unedifying reactions were thoroughly discontented ones and it appeared one hatch was leading and the others mimicking in order to dissuade the rebellious hatch from working with the capybara.

The capybara began to grow alarmed by this new tactic.

Also, the apparently rejuvenated leader of the hatches had the number 3 emblazoned on it, moved ferociously, opening and closing its hatch door rapidly like a ravenous predator would, when chomping on its prey.

Yet the one emitting a friendly, warm glow by his feet, also had a number on it, but it was flipped horizontally.

He moved closer, to this hatch and peered over the character — the other hatches began to rumbustiously make an extraordinary and aggressive clattering sound, as if they were rattled; the sound became like a cacophony of indescribable proportions and the capybara winced with the harshness of the sound.

"How was this possible?" he reflected with nerves now jangling on edge.

The tender hatch which was under his feet, was still gently nudging him and gritting his teeth and with perseverance etched all over his face, he looked intently for any key sign that this could indeed be the hatch to open.

His reluctance was understandable.

He tentatively moved the horizontally flipped number and as he nudged the metal plated number, it began to respond and the character swivelled around anti-clockwise, precisely one hundred and eighty degrees.

Thus, it was magically repositioned — and acknowledging its prominence, clicked the character into position, whereupon two letters reading "RR" gradually began to be seen in the bottom left-hand corner of the hatch.

Kerisay's heart leaped into the air with joy, as he recognised his mother's initials.

"I can't believe it," he asserted out loud, to which the reaction from the gang of hatches grew angrier and their crimson colour inclined further, so its red, green and blue mixture values, had slightly more than sixty percent red.

Kerisay reached out and pulled the handle of the gentle hatch and as a result, there was shocked silence emanating from within the edifice.

Sensationally, this precipitated a furious reaction from his nemeses.

This pack of hatches angrily realised that the capybara had made a decision and manically clattered and clashed with one another deliberately to illustrate their vexation.

Still in his own dreamland, he could see a ladder beneath him appear, which was different from what had been conveyed by his mother. But he trusted his instincts. As he dipped his head down first into the hatch's tunnel, the tunnel sensed his presence and gradually began straightening.

As he moved further securely forward, he realised at that precise moment, the hatch door behind him closed emphatically, to which he literally sped ahead oblivious to any commotion behind him.

Fascinatingly, the plain hatch nudged Kerisay, waking him out of his dream.

The young capybara dramatically opened his closed eyes. An exterior passiveness that he had exhibited had fortuitously and magically quelled the hatches.

With alarm bells ringing in his ears, he shook his head frenetically, revealing the exit tunnel's contours to the magic mirror, which would in turn lead inextricably on to his world. There was a blanket of fog, basically a barrier separating the Room of Hatches from the first tunnel.

He adventurously burst forward, triggering the inert and previously belligerent hatches into a belated raucous action. That inertia was costly!

The intense galloping raised his heartbeat and hopes, bringing him closer to what he believed was a familiar and homely light.

After breathing heavily, he stopped abruptly to check the location of the particularly troublesome hatches, who were too far away to cause difficulties. The instinct to succeed was inspirational and he bravely navigated on, thus surprising himself with his adroitness and new-found confidence.

Seeing the mirror in touching distance, he built up momentum... then leapt through, with his eyes closed.

The sound that brought the capybara through to his world, was a mighty and reverberating one. The structure of his home shook with a sigh of relief and the resonating vibration reached all parts of the house.

His eyes blinked and then opened wide in happiness.

Chapter 12 – A Resurgent and Rekindled Friendship

Following the further blinking of his eyes, Kerisay bounded downstairs from the first-floor landing. He did not want to lose any time, but on route, noticed that the library room door was still ajar, precisely at the angle it had been before his departure.

What's more, he did observe that the time of the day in his world had not elapsed. When he had first left his world, it was early evening and the clock hands on his return, were unchanged, precisely pointing to 6 pm (not a second later). The sun was still shining contentedly. Dashing downstairs, the food looked as delectable, as it had prior to his departure. Nothing had changed!

"It's weird in a sense, to see that time has stood still. This is perhaps a positive omen," contemplated Kerisay hopefully.

In his own and familiar surroundings, he was never one to beat around the bush and could be quite opinionated when the time was right.

Kerisay looked around for the final time, before charging out of the house. Naturally, he headed straight towards Zerisoyah's abode, via the inordinately long Capybara High Street. The home was actually owned by Zerisoyah's aunt.

He was surprised though, to see a perfectly cloudless sky, which was highly unusual at just after 6 pm. This appeared only very rarely.

In the meantime, Zerisoyah was with her twin sister in their expansive, immaculate and expensively manicured front garden.

They were briefly enjoying the idyllic weather and taking sips of fresh water to quench their thirst, from the wonderfully crafted wooden bowls, containing delicious sparkling water.

At this juncture, it is worth addressing that Zerisoyah and her twin generally kept themselves to themselves. Their parents had passed away and both sisters were reluctant to talk about their parents.

Of the twins, Merisoyah had reacted the worst and would shun company, except in the main, when communicating with her elder twin Zerisoyah.

Additionally, and as such, any mention of their parents, would cause the twins to clam up, indeed remain silent, tight-lipped for a long time afterwards... or alternatively, walk away, to avoid conversation and painful feelings.

The twins lived with their maternal aunt, who was called Werisoyah and had a lovely personality.

She was fabulously fun to be around. At the same time, the aunt was prone to literally laugh at the silliest, or the most trivial of situations — basically begin laughing at the drop of a hat.

This was perhaps a protective cover, as the aunt had a heart of pure gold. She doted on her nieces and was determined to shield them from sadness. Thus, laughter was a remedy to keep the twins from thinking about their beloved parents.

Therewith, the aunt was very aware of the circumstances surrounding the vanishing of her sister and brother-in-law. Werisoyah, like her younger sister felt that the C-Echelons were far too powerful and critical of dissent and kept on telling her younger sister to keep one's own counsel, but this became a bone of contention between them. Thereupon, Zerisoyah's sister and brother-in-law disappeared out of the blue. Rumours spread like wildfire that they had been imprisoned, or expelled to one of the scary adjacent islands.

Incidentally, Werisoyah never got to the bottom of the disappearance of her relatives, as she was frightened of what may be discovered, or the reactions of the despised C-Echelons.

Kerisay finally arrived at Werisoyah's home, breathing heavily, in a tired state of panic and forthrightly cried out, "Zerisoyah, help, help me!"

Zerisoyah hastily turned around, rotating elegantly 360 degrees and saw her friend racing up towards her, with newly laid turfs of grass in her aunt's front garden being flung up into the air.

"What's the matter? Wait... wait. Be careful of the grass," she opined in exasperation.

"Sorry, I need your help. Also, kindly excuse me if I appeared a little curt, when I saw you last... the time you generously came over to offer assistance. I should have been more appreciative."

"No need to thank me. That was in the past Kerisay. I don't hold grudges, but I sense there is something wrong. I'll also ignore the divots in the grass, shall I?" chirped Zerisoyah sarcastically, thinking she was being whimsical.

Merisoyah innately sensed anxiety in Kerisay and whispered into her sister's ear to show more support and hospitality. Displaying sensitivity was not always Zerisoyah's forte.

"Do not fret my dear friend," remarked Zerisoyah gently, which contrasted with her earlier demeanour and was conveyed in a soothingly measured tone, which was relatively surprising, one may perceive, in the circumstances.

"What I am about to say," continued Zerisoyah as her twin sister quietly left, "is that I can definitely help, but I also shall surprise and amaze you!"

Kerisay was taken aback by the confident words and that would be an understatement.

"Kerisay, I have… a gift like your mother, but she is more knowledgeable and experienced."

"Experienced in the gift?"

"Yes, she has tried to keep this island safe and be discreet. The protection enchantment was initiated by both your mother and maternal grandmother. Your mother's powers have properly ensured that the mendacious C-Echelons were, a safe distance from your family. Moreover, the deadly energy force that first emerged almost a hundred years ago and had recently caused so much damage, vehemently resurfaced!"

In all honesty, Kerisay found that this information was going far over his head.

"Alas, this conflict has aged your mother. Its return has distressed her. She is losing her memory and her powers. There are moments of brightness in her life, but she has really struggled to even manage certain finite situations.

"As such, she urgently wanted an assistant to pass on her spells. Not everyone gets to learn these spells by heart and it takes years. I have felt privileged," added Zerisoyah.

Kerisay's eyes remained open and his mouth was agape in wonder, as he absentmindedly blurted out mechanically, "Your… her assistant… and mother has a library, where she stores important items!"

"Thank you, my friend. I appreciate that. Also, your mother can control objects and other animals with her mind. Yet doing so is extremely exhausting, as is trying to particularly deter the dark energy force. Let us deal with the matter in hand now! Your father is in danger, as in your mother. I sense this."

"How will... you deal with matters?"

"I will endeavour. Can I add a caveat? As I said, I'm not as experienced as your mother, but I have learned a few of the spells, which will come in useful. They are inordinately long and I won't bore you with them!"

"I don't want to be rude, but I am bewildered and unsure how we can rescue my parents, if you know just a few spells? Which one will work?"

"Okay. Tell me, where is your father now?"

"He is in the human world and fled towards the river! He thought we had been in a different time period. That was my feeling. Perhaps, another dimension on Earth?"

"Did your mother leave any instructions?"

"Yes, we followed them, as best we could and it was only later that we thought the wrong hatch had been chosen."

"Okay. The spell I'll recite will emphatically clear from your father's mind, the cloud which was a curse emanating from the dark energy matter, known as SSK1. That dark energy has incredibly survived, like your mother for many, many years, but SSK1 has been tearing away at your mother's heart and soul throughout this seemingly endless period. It has caused her strife and sadness, though on the surface she has always been ebullient and shielded both you and your family."

"I miss my parents Zerisoyah," contemplated Kerisay.

"I can empathise with you. So, we must act. Let me fill you in and convey that the cumulative draining of energy is detrimental, for the protector, yet she has bravely guarded you and the island. The storm caused unspeakable damage allowing the energy form to escape and now it seeks evil ways to become omnipotent. To that end, there's a desire to disrupt your mother's life, whilst simultaneously seeking retribution for its imprisonment. It can find weaknesses and one weak link is prevalent and that means your father is unable to... perhaps."

"Just a second... that is wrong. There is no weak link. Also, this energy form is called what again?" interceded Kerisay in a surly and rapid tone, showing instant displeasure at the thought there was any criticism being levelled at his father, as well as instinctively displaying a sign of solidarity to his immediate family.

"Kerisay, please allow me to kindly clarify. SSK1 is the creature's infamous name. The battle with SSK1 is an historical one and sadly, may last forever. Also, I am sorry, if I hurt your feelings, when talking about your father. Your father is firstly, a fine capybara and very well respected. He has been naturally preoccupied with your grandmother's funeral, plus he is a skilled builder and received a garland for his professionalism. His work is greatly admired by everyone in our community."

"Thank you for the clarity Zerisoyah."

"Let me add, by saying that even so, learning any spell precisely takes hours and hours of practice, as you need to recite them without error and they must be perfect in every sense, intonation, feeling, preciseness, plus the more powerful ones, have to be spoken on a clear cloudless day, like we have today.

"Not everyone can learn these spells verbatim and that is not being conceited. Your mother has psychic powers… and could easily gain information as well as, of course, utilise pure positive energy to impact on the movement of objects."

"No way!"

"Yes, my friend. She does and genuinely believes that I have a gift too, which she wanted to develop… just in case anything happened to her. I am like her apprentice."

Kerisay was mulling over the last sentence.

"Likewise, I cannot detect, as yet, changes that are occurring far away, but if I encounter an individual animal face-to-face, even if they appear to be on the surface fine, then I can sense if they need any help, or if there is any tinge of sadness in their heart. Your mother and I seek only to bring peace, love and happiness to the hearts of others."

"We need to return to my home... now," urged Kerisay.

"Please... wait my friend."

Kerisay looked around mistily.

At that moment, Zerisoyah's twin appeared from out of nowhere, handing her a magnificently luxurious looking, silver coloured folder, before quietly returning to the inside of their house.

Zerisoyah, with the now open folder in her possession began briefly and quietly meditating. It was almost, as if she was absorbing crucial information, before intending to disclose pertinent facts.

Simultaneously, Kerisay duly noticed that Merisoyah had been effortlessly carrying a familiar looking small and pretty crossbody messenger bag, much like his mother's that was bigger on the inside than it was on the outside, which the twin had also deftly passed on to her sister's shoulder.

"This was your mother's folder and inside there are spells, which appear profuse to the naked eye and uneasy to assimilate, but they have been explained to me. I still have so much to learn. I understand that each presented spell is, to ultimately only assist others or for attaining a type of zen!

"Plus, she has given me some historical context of the island that at first, I found quite difficult to believe."

"A lot of what you are saying requires me to take stock. It is literally overwhelming."

"Since the last conflict ended almost 100 years ago, your mother, in her past life, had first managed to first repel the dark energy form and then magically contain it. However, she is from a certain line of unique capybaras, who have died out. But your mother is the last line of magicians and reawakens after every 25 years."

"Actually, how old is my… mother?" faltered Kerisay.

"Let me put it this way. She is in her Fourth Reawakening and I am so sorry to convey this to you… she is in her final awakenment, having been born on the 13th June in the year 2063. She realised that her powers in this fourth period of awakenment gradually diminish and she wanted to pass on her knowledge to me. She sensed that I had the potential to support her, in her time of need."

"I am struggling to put into words my inner thoughts. I... have so many questions, because to be frank, there is so much that I didn't know about my mother!"

"I will have to tell you more later. For the time being you will need to trust me. Listen my friend, this spell," as she turned the pages of the folder delicately, before continuing, "should... do the trick! This is... the stuff that will make the hair on your back stand on its end!"

"What will... happen now?" Kerisay remarked in a deadpan manner, as he overlooked his friend's humour.

"You will see... just wait... wait please," she stutteringly countered, more from a perspective of trying to simultaneously navigate through the folder, whilst speaking, before adding hastily, "the spell is called, Clearing Cloudy Minds and I believe it will work. Hopefully!"

"Oh I... see," observed Kerisay unconvincingly. He was used to Zerisoyah's sense of irony.

"This spell can be used, as your father was accursed and this impacted on you too, since you are his son. It is a cruel curse and needs lifting. It is intentionally blocking out what your father can actually see in the human world. Nevertheless, I promise we will get through this."

Zerisoyah proceeded in a palpably assertive voice to recite the spell.

A cloudy mind is not aligned,
Clearance, clearing, clearance, clearing,
A cloudy mind struggles to define.
Your embattled mind must change to an awakened mind.

A cloudy mind is not well-refined,
Clearing, clearance, clearing, clearance,
A decluttered mind must be your design.
You be must reminded to incorporate an organised mind.

Clear the mind, "lift the 'fog of war'",
"Is my song," uttered galore.
Now remove the deliberate curse,
Reject and repel, observe.
"The cloud is gone; all malcontent shall disperse!"

Kerisay stood in awe, whilst praying that matters would change at an instinct and that somehow his parents could be with him soon. There was a slight pause and as he opened one eye and then slowly the next, he could see Zerisoyah scratching her head.

"What's the matter?"

"Well… I don't think I recited the spell one hundred percent!"

"Sorry, you have not recited the spell correctly?" squirmed Kerisay in a hushed, but shocked sounding voice, as this was not the time for false promises.

"The spell has to be perfect and I should have raised my voice, whenever the word 'MUST' appeared. This is, of course Rolanda-Runa's spell. She is the author. I know... what have I have to do now. No more mishaps, hopefully!"

Zerisoyah judiciously corrected the spell and it was perfectly recited. Just then, there was a frightening crack of lightning.

"Run Kerisay, I have two more enchantments to deliver in advance. When they are stored in my mind, I can mentally access them at any time. It's quite useful. I shall catch up... trust me! SSK1 has spies and we need to move with haste."

"Trust you," repeated a pondering Kerisay to himself.

As he turned around towards home, he could hear Zerisoyah uttering the first of these spells to do with opening hatches.

Fill your mind with heroics
And not be just one hero, but many heroes.
Be a shimmering rainbow of light, as mysterious
As ctenophores.

So, beware of the Hatch
That is NOT numbered a simple 3.
It is a foe, burns duplicitously bright,
And is, here to deceive!

Instead, search calmly for the true Hatch you desire.
It'll warm your soul, seek help and then steer,
It's a friend, have a strange 3
That'll be fixed, 2 initials doth appear.

From a distance, Kerisay wistfully dreamed about his beloved home. He proceeded to gallop onwards and had no other thought in his mind than the welfare of his parents.

Just as he headed round the final corner of Capybara High Street in the direction of his home at number 3, Rolanda-Runa Road, he thought his mind was playing tricks, when he unexpectedly saw Zerisoyah, without her twin, leisurely approaching him.

"How did you get… here so fast?"

"It's just the Time Travel spell."

"Hang on a minute, do all these spells belong to my mother?"

"Yes, but there are countless more in her library."

"My mother can't properly use the spells Zerisoyah, whereas you can?"

"There is a reason. As I've said, your mother is now in her Fourth Reawakening and also as SSK1 had escaped, she was further weakened, after his last brutal island attack."

Kerisay nodded his head to convey that he understood.

"Her ability to precisely remember the spells became a problem. When they are not recited perfectly, it can cause a time disturbance and you may end up anywhere in the infinite and ever-expanding universe."

Kerisay, was literally stumped for words and frozen to the spot at his friend's ability and skills to elucidate. Zerisoyah was approximately his age, but she was knowledgeable far beyond her years.

Zerisoyah had also with great dexterity, whilst Kerisay was on his way home, swiftly extracted some of the spells from the silver folder, folded them carefully and carried them securely (so she thought), in the dainty, crimson coloured messenger bag.

Unfortunately, one particular spell she had not secured.

For the time being, the quieter sister Merisoyah knew what she had to do and remained at the aunt's home. She was reliable, trustworthy and silent. So long as there was quiet, the spies of the C-Echelons were uninterested in proceedings.

Chapter 13 – Kerisay Senior Reunited

Meanwhile, Kerisay Senior who had been hiding in fear, in the river and concealed under intense green and luxuriant foliage, whilst getting hungrier by the minute in this human world, was still filled with nerves.

What greatly worried the father was how long he would have to remain in the human world. The longer he stayed in this world, the less he liked it.

However, he ever so gradually began to realise, little by little that a strange sensation that had been clouding his mind, was lifting. It was a struggle he could have done without!

The clarity of thinking was more conspicuous.

At the same time, the humans who just earlier were looking agitated and talking noisily, were fortuitously and gradually losing interest in the fantastic animal footprints, as incessant rain seemed to arrive magically, washing away the last vestiges of the footprints. In no small measure, this was abetted by a distracting and reckless car incident in the nearby vicinity, which saw two skidding vehicles unable to keep their distance and collide dramatically. Fortunately, no human was hurt, but the noisy commotion drew an interested crowd.

Seeing his chance and double checking his immediate surroundings, Kerisay Senior cautiously left the river and hurried back in the direction of the imposing Java kapok tree. He was vigilant at all times.

The destined tree was massive, but as he walked briskly and circumvented its enormous girth, he could now for the first time recognise the house, with its unique ash grey coloured front door. There was not just an unkempt field.

It was a wonderful and cathartic sight!

What is more, he noticed the rain was still pouring down with increasing velocity and as he wiped away the water from his eyes, he saw a sight which lifted his heavy heart.

In front of him, was his beloved wife.

At that precious moment, they caught a glimpse of each other's eyes and galloped towards each other. It was a moment of unmitigated joy. Their eyes shone lovingly.

"Thank goodness I have found you my darling wife! For a while, I lost all hope. I have missed you enormously."

"I have missed you also dear husband."

"It has been a torture to remain in this world and I don't know how you have managed to cope Roland-Runa?"

"This human world is a dichotomy. There are some human leaders, who are self-centred to the detriment of the weakest and poorest in society. It is a world I want to leave, but I cannot. But to be fair, not all humans behave this way!"

"No, no, NO," cried out Kerisay Senior, focusing on the word cannot, before his tapering voice whispered, "this is a dream. This is not real. I cannot accept this catastrophe!"

"Please listen carefully my dear husband. What I will say will shock you, but it is true. This is my Fourth Reawakening. The spells I knew, I am finding it terribly difficult to recollect and also just reading them is becoming tougher by each passing day, because of my deteriorating eyesight and of course, the spells have been designed to be recited perfectly."

"We must be able to do something? Is there no way I can change your mind?"

"It is too late. I am aging and youthful magic is not eternal and importantly, I can't guarantee being precise anymore with my spells. Zerisoyah will be our new heroine."

"Is this all not a dream?"

"No, reality and the dream are one. If I travel back with you now, as I have reached almost the end of the Fourth Reawakening, it will be pointless. Over and above, the aging process was dangerously accelerated, due to the battle I had with the energy form during the terrible storm. SSK1 was manipulating Kerisay's mind and I had to help. The dark energy form has also been tearing away at me. If I can distract it, then that will be good. Also, Zerisoyah is trustworthy and she will be a fine defender of our world."

"But, won't SSK1 want to come to this human world and attack you?"

"That I cannot guarantee! An ancient enchantment had been placed to prevent it from causing havoc in other worlds. It was imprisoned, but the battle with the ancient wizard was ferocious and deadly. Now, the power needed to protect other worlds will be too great to harness. Only my mother and I survived from the line of wizards and she handed her powers to me. If my mother was still alive… we could possibly… stop SSK1 together."

The husband nodded his head in a manner, which was a sign of resignation. His beloved wife would not be returning with him.

"Beyond a shadow of a doubt, I sense that my young apprentice Zerisoyah will arrive soon and she will take you home. Look around you… there were footprints… they have disappeared. She has learned well and I am pleased with her. She will protect you and our world from SSK1."

"My wife, what will become of me? You are everything."

"Life is such. If I return now, I will be unrecognisable. I know that in this world, I may be able to do a little good in the last few days of my life… I can only try."

"But, if you are losing your memory, how can you still help these humans?"

"They are peculiar creatures. I try to write down words in their language, which is sometimes impossible or preferably use symbols, which I leave behind on their tables. A few of them have reacted positively, others have ripped the paper apart and growled angrily. I convey the importance of treating others with kindness and love. Showing respect, politeness and humility are universal values. I can only hope and pray they will heed the advice."

As they spoke, they could hear the great Java kapok tree swaying. Its branches moved dexterously and its leaves shielded the capybaras.

"There is something happening," observed Kerisay Senior.

"It's time my husband," whereupon she glided back a few paces to collect the cage containing the guinea pig Jettison.

The cage was entirely covered with tarpaulin and possessed a large handle, which had been prepared earlier at the human home. The preparation had been meticulously undertaken.

"Are you ready to return home dear Jettison and challenge the rulers?" Rolanda-Runa whispered to her friend.

"Yes, I shall be glad. It has been… a long, long time. I have greatly missed my world and my friends. Earth has not been an agreeable experience!"

"Do not worry. My apprentice is learning fast and she will return you to the original Second Reawakening form."

"I hope so Rolanda-Runa," was Jettison's measured reply.

The wife smiled lovingly at her husband and handed him the cage, before confiding, "Jettison's age has not changed!"

Jettison was aware that this time he would finally, return to his world to determine, if he had been betrayed to SSK1.

In the meantime, Zerisoyah had with unsurprising alacrity charged into Kerisay's house, with the latter trailing not far behind. Being young and not greatly experienced, as far as adventurers were concerned, they tried to take stock of the situation as best they could. The next stop was the mirror!

At first, the mirror was incandescent with rage, shaking and emitting a rumbustious sound of continuous glass breaking. This was an aggressive response to Kerisay, who in an ill-advised attempt to speed up the process to enter the mirror, had carelessly not recited the correct spell accurately. It had been hurried and filled with unbridled emotion. Nonetheless, every cloud has a silver lining and with Zerisoyah's mature patience, skilled assistance, as well as reassurance, they had subsequently and successfully repeated the enchantment with preciseness. The mirror then belatedly, accepted the two intrepid capybaras.

For a while, it was touch and go, as one may have correctly assumed the need for timeliness in the face of urgency.

In these circumstances, entering the magic mirror from their world, was fraught with danger and literally undertaken by the skin of their teeth, especially if one was to consider the pursuant tracker's proximity.

Having overcome this particular and initial hurdle, fortune had belatedly favoured the brave capybaras.

The entry into the Room of Hatches had been accomplished next, due in no small measure, to the determination and mental resourcefulness of the young capybaras. It appeared that she was finally fulfilling her undoubted potential.

Be that as it may, both she and Kerisay had not accounted for the dastardly scheming of SSK1.

Chapter 14 – SSK1 Returns

Indeed, SSK1 had nefariously sensed through its spies (the treacherous C-Echelons) that manipulating the storm and the ensuing pummelling had not been quite a resounding success. There was something amiss and SSK1 would never at all, let sleeping dogs lie.

From a distance, the sinister SSK1 had tracked the capybara adventurers and done so surreptitiously.

After the capybaras had left their world, through the magic mirror, the energy form had secretively pursued them, with stealth and speed.

Thus, facing adversity, the encountered mirror had been cowed into pitiful submission and thoroughly overwhelmed by the sheer omnipotent presence of SSK1. The mirror meekly accepted the cruel energy form's rite of passage, without even a whimper. SSK1 had subjugated the mirror and crushed its independence, through its immense willpower.

Meanwhile, the two intrepid capybaras cautious traverse into and access of the Room of Hatches, had seen them barely ahead of the agitating, pursuing and quickening SSK1.

Though, the young adventurous friends had entered quietly, almost as if they were mice; they stood still like ice statues and were completely mesmerised, for a few precious moments by the spectacular dimensions of the pyramid shaped room. That pause was a dangerous one.

The spectacular scene, specifically appeared to deluge Zerisoyah's mind.

Beleaguered and fatigued this young apprentice, was now feeling the effects of the pressure to succeed and the weight of expectations was gradually taking its toll.

Misgivings were preoccupying her and there was a sense that she was not one hundred percent confident to perfectly recite any of the spells verbatim, with all the negative connotations involved. Qualms were surfacing, through shifting movements and uncertain steps.

Undoubtedly, she was enduring doubts, second thoughts and worse.

"Let's please continue, we have no alternative. I believe in you. You are my only hope," passionately and bravely urged Kerisay, as he identified cold feet on behalf of Zerisoyah.

This level of friendly encouragement, lifted the apprentice's heart, soul and mind, reigniting her burning inner desire to prevail.

It prompted Zerisoyah to show even greater courage and opening her messenger bag, she deftly lifted the appropriate spell to counter the frightening situation.

"This is the one we need… hopefully… it will work," she confirmed with a semblance of more self-assuredness.

"Wait, there is something else in this room, with us... I feel its presence," uttered Kerisay in a state of bewildered fear.

"I am HERE," was the deep and menacing voice, which accompanied a shadow that came scarily into view.

Suddenly, all the hatches came to life and began moving around frantically. Their noise was deafening, as the dastardly voice and presence had unnerved them. The disorientated hatches covered the pictures on the side of the room shaped pyramid and navigated manically around the candles. The hatches fearfully hovered around and made irrationally loud clanking noises, colliding with each other in the process. Kerisay had never experienced anything like this before.

"Is there a spell to trap this energy form?" cried Kerisay in desperation.

"I don't know," as Zerisoyah unconvincingly fiddled in her messenger bag. The spells began falling out randomly, at which point the presence of the deadly creature laughed haughtily and with contempt.

SSK1 sniggered, "There is no way-out capybaras!"

Magically and at that point, one spell fell agonisingly close to Zerisoyah's feet and drifted over to her. She gasped. It was the X-Entity one.

"Whatever it is read it," pleaded Kerisay.

"No, NO," was the monstrous retort from SSK1, as it menacingly approached the young capybaras.

But as the young apprentice was vocalising the X-Entity spell, there was another enchantment, which was protruding in her bag. It was the Time Travel for One.

In the confusion, she had not entirely secured the bag. This was a disastrous mistake of potentially epic proportions.

In spite of this, as Zerisoyah began reading X-Entity, each hatch began automatically approaching the creature. The hatches reacted in sustained fury and shook the foundations of the room.

The candles began raining down and some pictures began cracking into haphazard and tiny pieces. The remaining faces on the pictures changed from contentedness to incandescent rage.

But was it too late... for SSK1?

The plethora of hatches descended upon the energy form and they all surrounded it. The hatches opened even more agitated, each and every one of them. Hundreds of them.

As they did, a miniscule unit of the creature's energy began peeling away from its being and entering each one of these hatches, which in turn closed its individual hatch door.

"NO! No," cried SSK1.

The dark energy form, tried to galvanise what was left of its energy and the battle raged on. Repelling the hatches appeared inadequate, as they had the strength of an army.

Terribly fortuitous, the evil entity had glimpsed the unsecured spell in Zerisoyah's bag and with venomous arrogance he cackled, "Come spell to me, come to me know."

Whilst all of this was transpiring, one plain looking hatch, which had the initials RR on it, had already and gently glided up to the feet of the capybaras. Its sweet, nudging warmth was noticeable, whereupon its hatch door opened immediately and without a second thought the capybaras jumped in.

Witnessing the episode, SSK1 violently dispersed some of the hatches away, but there were too many to simultaneously fight. It was still being overwhelmed and corralled. Trapped.

It was as if, each hatch was incredibly siphoning parts from the entity. Each separated part would be automatically sent to a different world. Some hatches were gateways to galaxies so far away that they would be impossible to reach within any lifetime. SSK1 knew that its hope for escape and survival would be impossible… unless its energy was directed towards one hatch.

The deceitful hatch.

It would mean that SSK1 could enter the human world, only weaker and more vulnerable.

On the other hand, imagine the possible insurmountable trouble it could still cause to a place that was already filled to the brim with war and sadness?

The dark energy creature laughed wickedly and then extolled conceitedly, "Yes, perhaps in a few years, I could regain my power and find a way back to seek revenge on the pitifully hapless capybaras, but at least there would be a new place I could call home. Planet Earth!"

The entry into the human world could be at any random time period, unless elucidated.

Yet the unsecured spell, was tantalisingly in reach and could specify the destination. Though greatly weakened, the vain energy form still myopically believed in its restitution!

Simultaneously, the two resolute capybaras rushed through the hatch tunnel's passage way leading inexorably to the Java kapok tree, whereupon they burst out into the human world.

As apparitions — first, Kerisay and then Zerisoyah, joyfully arrived, filled with hopeful expectations, for a triumphant rescue.

The rain was still billowing down on Earth. Roads were getting even more heavily flooded, people were rushing around in consternation and the river had burst its banks.

Suddenly, out of nowhere and to his delight, Kerisay saw his mother and with unadulterated glee ran towards her. The reunion was touching and they rested their heads against each other in sign of deep affection.

The mother stepped back and tearfully looked at her young female apprentice, "Thank you Zerisoyah for arriving… we are so very grateful."

"It is no problem at all Rolanda-Runa. It is my pleasure. I sense our meeting may be very short though," replied Zerisoyah.

"You are right and I have explained to my husband, as to why I need to stay" extolled the mother, as her son's attentive face changed from happiness to unimaginable despair.

"No mother, you cannot stay here! Come home, please," implored Kerisay, whose heart was breaking.

"I have no choice my son. Take Jettison and flee back to your world. Sadly, I sense, SSK1 will arrive in this world and there will be even more conflict and misery. I need to make sure he never departs Earth."

"Mother, I beg you to leave with us... I will stay and fight with you. Together, we will be stronger!"

"My time is near, my dear son. I am in the Fourth Reawakening and therefore, I can't depart. The magic necklace was no more, with no capacity of note, sadly indicating the power was draining from me. The travelling to and from different worlds has weakened me further, plus I lost so much energy over the decades, in trying to contain SSK1. I miserably failed... miserably."

"No there was no failure," interrupted Zerisoyah. "You are a heroine; your name will reverberate for all eternity."

"I already have a town named after me in this human world, though I have to find out why... please go. I implore you."

The husband and son looked at Rolanda-Runa and wept bitter tears.

"Please don't grieve... you don't have much time left. Go now... you will always be in my thoughts, prayers and in my hopes for all eternity."

"We need to go now," urged Zerisoyah, as she turned to look into the eyes of the husband and his son, who nodded meekly.

Rolanda-Runa turned her back. She walked very slowly and sadly away, as the rain cascaded down.

"I shall read the last spell, but all three of us must join minds to form a three-dimensional triangle, for the Time Travel spell to work. If not, we are in big, BIG trouble… only joking," added Zerisoyah with a hint of bravado, which did not go down too well.

"Forgive me. My attempt at humour can be misplaced… hold tight… the spell is now in sight… alright!"

At this point, Kerisay Senior, Kerisay and Zerisoyah, were all together, swept with alacrity into the tree, based on age seniority. Jettison followed looking quite alarmed.

Travelling at lightning speed and into the Room of Hatches, circumnavigating around the belligerently disbelieving SSK1 and then onwards towards their freedom.

They collectively crashed through the mirror, which began slowly shattering into a shower of a thousand fragments. There would be no homecoming for Rolanda-Runa now.

"SSK1 surely won't return to our world again…," Zerisoyah exultantly asserted, but it was tinged truth be told, with just a miniscule of doubt.

The capybaras placed their three heads together out of a sign of mutual respect and relief that they were safely in their own world.

In the far distance, they could hear the shocking shriek of SSK1, whose energy had been depleted and pulled asunder.

From its vindictive perspective, the humiliatingly departure from the Room of Hatches would be rightfully avenged.

Yet, whatever semblance remained of SSK1, it deviously appeared, incredibly so, whilst clutching the stolen spell, to be miraculously heading in the direction of the human world. The day of arrival on Earth, would be Monday 9th May, in the year 2163. The time was set for 3 pm.

Travelling in the opposite direction, the creature's remorseless voice was traumatically harsh and beseechingly frightful, "NO Containment spell! Planet Earth, let me roam and sow seeds of your destruction! Rolanda-Runa... can you not hear? Won't you hear me?"

Painfully, as the creature's fading voice echoed into the distant realm, a final protestation and spine-tingling reckoning followed, "Your ancestor... was cruel to me. His sorcery and punishments... were horrendously unjust Rolanda-Runa. I was his... apprentice! My return will be replete, with a furious vengeance. Just you wait... and see!"

Surely, two old adversaries would be destined to meet once again and of course, their fate was inextricably entwined.

Chapter 15 – Soliloquy

It is the Siren-Spirit-King-One.
"I AM SSK1," I scream with passion.
It felt like eternity; I was in prison
And this injustice won't be forgiven.

I was once a humble individual,
Yet the wizard felt I was ineffectual.
I pleaded, "This is not fair!"
Yet, admonishment came, he couldn't care.

What have I done to deserve this?
I believed my world was bliss.
But there was a moment's change
And the wizard could rearrange.

But, "I am unclear" about a mistake,
Did I speak out of turn, or cause heartache?
Now every utterance is a plague!
The spell to contain the FBS vague?

The wizard roared, "I cannot trust",
Spitting hatefully with disgust!
"But you asked me to help?" I cried.
Then, he turned his back, as if to deny.

As, I left the scene in heartache,
His rage shook, was like an earthquake.
"Return now or be damned",
Or try to solve a fateful anagram.

"What tomfoolery is this?" I pleaded.
An anagram for "FILE" is heeded.
Does this mean a prison's LIFE?
"Yes," he said, "you'll suffer endless strife!"

I am told that a cave shall seal,
Me, plus my "treacherous" friends will kneel.
There is an error, I refuse to subjugate.
"You will ACCEPT don't obfuscate!"

My form is altered,
Listen to me, my shaking heart falters.
My mind is blank, my soul is bereft
Taken, broken, this is a cruel theft!

The "wise" wizard conveniently forgot,
That I was an apprentice too and could retort.
I escaped and surprised,
He snarled untruly that I connived.

The battle raged, the tussle would not end,
I said, "You're mistaken again and again!"
It was jealousy and foolish pride,
The other capybaras would snigger and hide.

Finally, the spell I was placed under,
Was exacted with hatred and thunder.
This time for me, there was no escape
And the wizard departed, with mouth agape!

By Hess Moontasir

Time passed and I remained trapped,
In a state of limbo, my energy capped.
A year elapsed, then nigh a century too,
Serendipitously, a lifeline, came into view.

The storm arrived on the capybara world,
It tore and shredded, then did unfurl,
A potent power that I could harness.
At last was free, sensed complete catharsis.

The capybaras sped, fled, filled with dread,
"We're alone and vulnerable", it was spread.
Yet my spies were faithful to the end,
My knowledge gained, I shall portend.

But, a wizard's scion with insolence,
Fought, with foolish resilience.
Mightily, I determined what to peruse,
Who to consider, use and thus pursue?

Now, verily here, on a place called Earth,
To bide time, then take control, with mirth.
Still Rolanda-Runa, may show some anguish,
If we meet; I'll flourish, publish with relish!

As I wait, I do merrily hypothesise,
The torment is fresh, seek no compromise.
If I ever shall "reminisce" in vain,
At once I'll know, what finally, will remain!

Earth is interesting, it can be strange,
Humans walk and talk, then become estranged.
At times they may invite, others just fight,
So, stealthily Earth may be conquered at night!

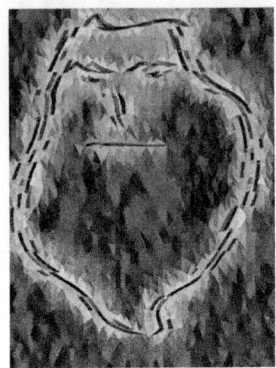

# Chapter 16 – Rolanda-Runa's Farewell

Rolanda-Runa is my pseudonym,
A melancholy farewell, uttered grim.
To my dear family and dearest friend,
Your company I'll not share again.

The storm arrived, 25th April 2163,
It was destructive, mean and not a dream.
Consequences truly shocking to behold,
Damaging life, structure, hope, left me cold.

Initially unsure of the storm's deadly causes.
Perturbed I was, there would be no applauses.
Animals fled in fear, scurried behind,
Nature's protectors, but torment was blind.

My husband and son were truly alone,
Trapped, bullied storm's source unknown.
Managed to escape and be taken home,
To be with loved ones, but my mind did roam.

My spell had worked, the storm had eased,
But weakened — my powers felt seized.
There was an energy form I began to sense,
From long ago, my other name, a defence.

Now, a spell entered my dear son's mind,
A foreboding dream that was so unkind.
Only one individual could have that effect,
My heart knew, the dark energy to deflect.

Told my son that this dream I would take,
I would leave my home, two worlds at stake.
For a time, he'd endure a knowledge gap,
An honest appraisal and never a trap.

When the time in May to depart my world,
Knew the speed of change would not be furled.
But, a young apprentice with such skill and sense,
Received my knowledge on the ninth day hence.

Finally, Kerisay became fully aware,
Of salient messages; issued with care.
Our library would be a source of all power,
Stacked, silver cubes, as tall as a tower.

From the critical point on,
Data transmitted, then gone.
Leave no single trace for the deadly energy,
But usher the loved, create mental synergy.

The mirror knew me, I entered on time,
Which fortunately was, an encouraging sign.
The movement forward, the Room of Hatches,
A set of challenges, no untimely despatches!

Moving deftly and precisely,
Approached the prescribed hatch wisely.
The gentle warmth emitted,
Triggered door opening — committed.

By Hess Moontasir

Eventually, I saw the human world,
Strange but true, with banners that unfurl.
Showing messages, protests, strikes and more,
Conflict resolutions they appear to abhor.

Discovered Jettison's home, locked in prison.
He was our friend, skilful with vision.
Betrayed by dark magic, via C-Echelon spies,
Their thirst for power, with deceitful eyes.

In the meantime, my husband and son,
Determined bravely to not be undone,
Followed me to this planet, called Earth.
Convinced my aching heart, this has worth!

Solemnly, from what I did learn,
SSK1's rising power was a concern.
My husband's world turned upside down,
Accursed, abandoned, another town.

My son returned from the human place,
Courageous elation was etched on his face.
My apprentice was ready and full of verve,
To take my mantle, intrepid, to justly deserve.

The adventurous youngsters rushed back,
Collected my husband, my friend, were on track.
To magically hone in on my real home,
Ensuring mirror's end, no longer to drone.

Recognising that I shall remain on Earth,
For this is my "penance" for all that's worth!
Endeavour, redeem people's destiny,
Perhaps "spirits" squash SSK1's enmity.

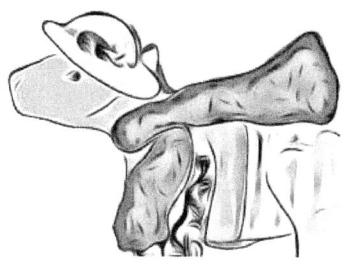

Appendix – A to Z of Rolanda-Runa's Spells

The following spells are a sample of the vast collection Rolanda-Runa, at one time possessed and which she could recite to perfection.

Most of her enchantments are located in the family's amazing library.

Amalgamation with Love

Apply the following, if a family member is far apart and the aim is having them reunited with the ones they love.

Arrange the magical stars,
Coalesce signs near and far.
If you feel pain, or the door's ajar,
Then, just be calm and
Set the bar.

No matter how far apart,
Look intensely at your heart.
You'll find the one who is dear,
And soon reunite and
Be glad to cheer.

Bag Protector

Deploy this enchantment, when the contents of the dainty crimson messenger bag, containing the silver folder of spells you are carrying, needs protection from an evil eye.

Spells in crimson bag,
Be safe and secure!
Each one is precious
And each will endure.

An indomitable bag,
All spells neatly bound.
In a silver folder —
Signed RR — renowned.

A dark as night heart
Is one that's not true.
So, an evil eye,
Will never sneak through.

Spells — be safe from,
Prying, spying, conniving eyes.
Repeat, "I keep secure,
In the folder, where you reside".

Bouncy Boisterous: A Shining Sun.

To be only utilised when the capybara is feeling low, after having a duller than dull day.

Of course, there is no recourse,
That's how it might be seen (at source),
When the dullest of a grey day,
Is refusing to give the light its way.

And the awful time will end surely,
When you a hear a friendly voice, calling purely.
To forget the pining, see the sun shining,
So, there is always a silver lining.

A joyfulness that raises one's heartbeat,
Be ebullient, dance and stomp your feet,
Live life, love and prosper, see the sun shining.
So, there is always a wonderful silver lining.

Clearing Cloudy Minds

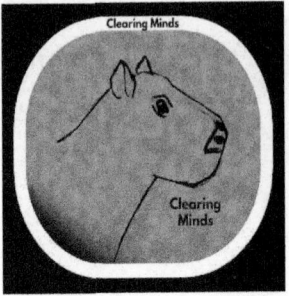

If a curse to sow confusion, has been placed on the recipient, then use this spell to clear the individual's cloudy mind.

A cloudy mind is not aligned,
Clearance, clearing, clearance, clearing,
A cloudy mind struggles to define.
Your embattled mind MUST change to an awakened mind.

A cloudy mind is not well-refined,
Clearing, clearance, clearing, clearance,
A decluttered mind MUST be your design.
You MUST be reminded to incorporate an organised mind.

Clear the mind, "lift the 'fog of war'",
"Is my song," uttered galore.
Now remove the deliberate curse,
Reject and repel, observe.
"The cloud is gone; all malcontent shall disperse!"

Containment

Can only be used twice, when a dangerous energy form has to be contained.

To you dark shadow and to you alone,
I contain your awful energy.
Without compromise, or hesitation,
I shall deploy the last vestiges of power.
From the Great Wizard's memory.
Reap dark shadow what you sow!
Thou shall be no hope, no remedy.

To you, dark shadow and to you alone.
This is MY eternal... WISH,
To see your malignant malignancy,
Restrained, contained, sealed hermetically.
Nullified, trapped, demystified.
SSK1, duly disqualified,
This I do — verily verified.

Demanding Decisions

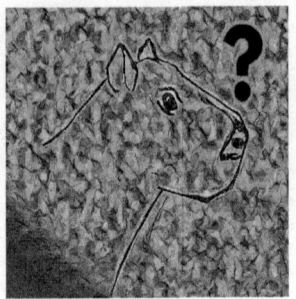

You are at work and need to show kindness and support to others, though you are under considerable stress.

Sometimes decisions are tough,
Occasionally the outcomes may be rough.
Others may well hypothesise, empathise, sympathise;
Thus, you are not alone.
Don't feel... all there's left is to moan.

However, be kind and reassuring,
Show gentleness and be unassuming.
You will win their hearts and their minds,
Contentedness will hereafter reign
And importantly... you won't be sad or drained.

Effervescent Feelings

If you are playing sport and wish to obtain and maintain a sense happiness whilst playing the sport.

Keep those effervescent feelings,
No need to think they'll be fleeting.
Be reassured and play your chance.
Show strength and exuberance.

There may be ups and downs,
Highs and may be slumps.
But you may come out a champ,
Honourable, worthy and not a scamp!

Fun, Fun, Fun

You are at a party and really wish to have a fun time with family and friends (though you feel a little rundown from a hard day at work).

The day has been inordinately laborious,
It's a drag and there's been behaviour,
Witnessed that has veered... between
Two polar extremes and quite frankly... the riotous.

Certainly, you are not a bore, but a kind-hearted soul,
Nonetheless it's pointless to just: work and work.
Life's too short, so have: fun, fun, FUN!
You're venerable, ambitions, completely whole.

Galvanising: Go Away, Go Away, Go Away.

When there is present or existential danger, recite the following.

Incidentally, the Beacon of Sear was a special staff the ancient capybara wizard used, to emit an intense light.

When there is danger, elude the frightful fear.
When there's foreboding, it's all too clear.
So, galvanise yourself into being strong,
To stand tall and be proud,
Let the words ring out volubly and loud.

Galvanise, move with rapidity,
Revitalise, be alert, show alacrity.
Rationalise, motivate, no need to subjugate.
Apprise, rise, use your mind, do not abate.
Face your fear and be a Beacon of Sear.

Reiterate to the foe, "GO AWAY".
Yes, live to fight another day.

Hatch Opener

Used to safely navigate through the Hatch challenge. There are two versions. The second shorter one, is useful when time is of the essence.

Version 1

Fill your mind with heroics
And not be just one hero, but many heroes.
Be a shimmering rainbow of light and as mysterious
As ctenophores.

Be careful, quiet and calm,
Once you enter the Room of Hatches,
No rousing alarm, for they'll be reticent
With no axe to grind and easy despatches.

Yet, beware of the Hatch
That is NOT numbered a simple 3.
It's a foe, burns bright, a friend of SSK1
And is here, here to deceive!

Au contraire, search calmly for the Hatch you desire.
It'll warm your soul, seek help and then steer.
It's a friend, have a strange 3
That'll be fixed, 2 initials shall appear.

Version 2

Fill your mind with heroics
And not be just one hero, but many heroes.
Be a shimmering rainbow of light, as mysterious
As ctenophores.

So, beware of the Hatch
That is NOT numbered a simple 3.
It is a foe, burns duplicitously bright,
And is, here to deceive!

Instead, search calmly for the true Hatch you desire.
It'll warm your soul, seek help and then steer,
It's a friend, have a strange 3
That'll be fixed, 2 initials doth appear.

Instinct Irredentist

The enemy has been contained or repelled and there's now a need to restore the land to the true victims, not the C-Echelons.

Instinct irredentist,
Victory charm — with a tone that's evenest.
Is this existentialist threat for all?
Some may object, such as the elegist?

"Restore, reunite, reignite and overcome",
Is the speaker's victory thrum!
Repel false C-Echelon pretences, who foully,
Where purple robes — dyeing that's alum.

Joust Dance

There is a remarkable dance that the capybaras engage in. This is an activity that is taken very seriously and is called Joust Dance.

At the end of every year is a famous festival, which is called "The Annual Capybara Celebration", which involves the Joust Dance.

Joust Dance,
Be tenacious and you are out of sight.
Step to the left and step to the right,
Shake you left foot and then again, ALRIGHT!

Dance and joust
No need to feel at all contrite,
If you win then take a bow and fly a kite.
Dance merrily under the magical moonlight.

Joust Dance,
Be unflinching and you're not out of depth.
Step to the right and step to the left,
Shake you right foot and hold your BREATH!

Kilter Remedy

If you feel uncomfortable, which is causing an imbalance in your mind and heart, this may be the direct result of another's jealousy or actions towards you.

You will need to recite this enchantment, in order to present a sense of inner equilibrium and generate peacefulness and calm around you.

There are ups and downs,
There are bumps and frowns,
And those that act like awful clowns.

Who change sides, at the drop of a hat,
Facile faces, aimlessly chat.
Repel them fair, no need for combat.

Those who cause disturbance, converse to anesthetise.
Who say one thing and won't rationalise,
Who trivialise, want to sensationalise.

They care not one iota... but I ameliorate,
So be at peace, not act with haste.
Respond forthrightly, be calm, don't hesitate.

Loud Noise Reduction

After a night of partying that may continue for days, during the holiday season, capybaras tend to get quite loud. This spell helps to switch the mind off and reduce the noise intake, so other important activities may be undertaken.

The noise is so, VERY loud,
An over the top sound from a boisterous crowd.
Let there be a magical shroud,
To cover my ears and to soundly disavow.
It's not that I'm a party poop or really rude.
I've much work to do; don't want to be glued,
To activity that'll interminably last, be imbued.
An island protector's job never ends – that's news!
I can't afford to be tired or terribly confused.
I'll be focused and on task, in tune.

Munch your Lunch

Sometimes there may be a long work assignment that will prevent you from taking a proper or well-deserved break and this spell will help you fit your work in and also eat well at lunchtime.

Working, walking, working, walking.
Talking, planning, shifting, standing!
It is so exhausting,
Lifting, carrying, processing, invoicing,
Moving, shifting, turning, organising!
It is so consuming.

I will have a break, a deserved interval,
A refreshing cool drink, from a pitcher that's full.
"Plus, a quick mouth-watering salad sandwich,"
Heavenly spirits… hear my reasonable language!

Nauseous Feeling Remedied

To recover quickly after falling ill, which could be the result of too much partying or excessive work! This spell will help you to recover quickly.

What has happened?
What has happened?
I'm unsteady, unready,
That's no use, I'm really giddy!

Kind heavenly spirits release my woe,
From my head to my toes.
Flick the switch, now predict!
Quickly lift the illness that inflicts.

Protecting Protector

This can be used when you are away from home and need to protect your family.

If I am away for any length of time,
My heart is near and that is my paradigm.
Listen intensely to my voice, just fine.
It's not dull, nor dreary.
It's clear, not weary.

My spell... will protect you all,
A shield automatically... installs.
No threat will be invoked or called,
Safe from vituperative villainous villain
Or deadly miscreant cabal, no chilling!

Quaint: Honest Values

To be only used when trying to help others procure food and get a good bargain.

*Capybaras often say that life's a grapple,
Family, work and life's a stressful juggle.*

*If you are struggling to feed your family,
I'll help, fear not, no formality.*

*I kid you not, by virtue of no exaggeration,
There's honest help, no corrupt inflation.*

Righteousness (or Rightly Compromised)

You sometimes have to try and exaggerate a little to help others, who are in honest difficulty (perhaps they are trying to get into their sports team or need a helping hand). Using this spell will ensure that those in control will listen.

Most upright, moral and true;
You are in a back to the wall situation.
But I help, no problem, no hoodoo.

No deception. To you I say my friend,
Just a little help can go a long way.
No ulterior motive, no demeaning ends.

It is to progress, honestly help.
You're at your wits end.
Listen, have faith, don't yelp!

Successful Energy Repellent

Only to be used, if there are dark energy form is in the vicinity (such as SSK1).

Move swiftly, move with nous,
Don't be fooled, aims to educe

A quick understanding of the situation
Aware of a universal predation.

Consider the very next move,
And you'll need to countermove.

Successfully repel the energy form,
Come rain, or shine, or hailstorm.

Time Travel for One

Use this spell to carry you forward to different worlds and time periods, at the drop of a hat.

If you need is to travel
And journey... back or forth... through time,
Repeat the following stanza once, ever so fine...
Read slowly... because its divine.
Remember to pause to make it less anodyne.

Time Travel, Time Travel, Time Travel,
Travel unravel... identify channel 1...
[Name the time traveller]
[Place the day, month, year and time of arrival here]
Travel unravel... identify channel 1...
[Name the time traveller]
[Place the day, month, year and time of arrival here]

Need to be precise and opine,
Concise and please don't whine,
[Place the day, month, year and time of arrival here]
It's clearly not that radical!
Be precise — Time Travel Portal Prism is fragile!

Time Travel for Three

Consider this spell to carry you and two other companions, forward to different worlds and time periods, at the drop of a hat.

If you need is to travel
And journey... back or forth... through time,
Repeat the following stanza once, ever so fine...
Read slowly... because its divine.
Remember to pause to make it less anodyne.

Time Travel, Time Travel, Time Travel,
Travel unravel... identify channel 3...
[Name the time travellers]
[Place the day, month, year and time of arrival here]
Travel unravel... identify channel 3...
[Name the time travellers]
[Place the day, month, year and time of arrival here]

Need to be precise and opine,
Concise and please don't whine,
[Place the day, month, year and time of arrival here]
It's clearly not that radical!
Be precise, else Time Travel Portal Prism is fragile!

If its three of you that need to travel,
Minds together, a triangle form, no need for cavil.
Don't gaze back in anger or forward in desire,
No distractions needed, I won't misfire.
[Place the day, month, year and time of arrival here]

Turnip Race

This is a fun activity that families and friends partake in. Capybaras from within their respective region, congregate and use their skill to navigate between hundreds of turnips in a field.

A cup is awarded to the fastest capybara who runs around the turnip course.

The ultimate aim of this spell is to ensure that the entire event is conducted in harmony, as capybaras can be very competitive and whine if things don't go their way.

This is our prized Turnip Cup
For the new, old and the pups.

Everyone laughs, everyone will enjoy,
This spell means no one's annoyed.

Harmony and happiness prevail,
There is no bitterness and no discord,

There is no pretext, pretence, no tricky trail.
No participant is abhorred nor gets bored!

Urgent Rain

When there is a need for immediate rain, to alleviate the heatwave, this spell will be most beneficial.

Heatwave, severe, intense,
Can we end this pretence?
And allow a moment's rest,
To be at peace — I do attest.

High humidity, or blazing heat
That shall accrete.
Protect from harmful rays —
Interminably lasts for days.

Our inner sanctum, a plead for rain.
Bring showers, again and again.
No longer parched or terribly drained.
Plead for atmospheric change.

Victory with Compassion

Use this spell when the opponent in a game has been defeated, but remember to show warmth and compassion, so there is no enduring enmity.

Victory is a treat,
Not at all bitter sweet.
When emotions run high,
Feelings, tearful eyes dry.

Offer your hand in friendship.
You have won fair and square,
Withal, be aware
Always time to spare,

To treat others favourably
With compassion, with care.
"Happiness prevails" —
Is what I shall declare.

Weather Restrained

Utilise when the weather is so fierce that it is causing a disruption to capybara life.

I stand before you,
The Five Elements that are true.
Two in particular: air and sky,
So beautiful, through and through.

Stop this trouble and I
Humbly ask not why?
We are creatures that
Live in peace, wish fairly to comply.

Protect our world,
Ethereal ambience, it's testimony.
We're with you... not in discord,
But serenely, in perfect harmony.

X-Entity

This is a spell when the name of a dangerous entity, be it an inanimate or animate opponent, but not a capybara, is close at hand. So, you just wish that anyone, who encounters this entity called X will be protected.

Who is the X-Entity?
I have been given little information.
I'm to guess, yet provide security.

A donation, inflation, deflation or migration.
Or perhaps it's just an "individual",
Preparing to strike, hide its insidious location?

Protect requested one from this entity,
Who encounters this X?
Have my shield, protected against enmity.

"So, there are repercussions," I countered,
"It is you I detest."
A deadly, nefarious X, a malicious who else?
No requests, just prevail the ultimate quest!

"Go far away, you are not welcome here!"
I deride, demand and bray.
"Be gone disappear, be trapped"
And our fear shall be allayed.

Youthfulness Through Generation

At the end of each magical generation phase, remember to initiate the special words to remain young for the next 25 years. Only applies to those not in the Fourth Reawakening.

Gaze at the magic mirror, count to three!
Slowly: 1...2... and... 3.
Recite carefully, error free,
"I am virtuous" — say with glee!

Carefully without fear or favour, repeat
The following words, but don't bleat!
"Magic mirror, magnifying, magnificent
Majestic, metamorphosis, omnificent.
Reawaken, create me anew,
Forsake me not, agree to purview."

*"Please reawaken, so my old age
Disappears, I plead, I assuage.
Slowly: 1...2... and... 3,
Young again, this is no dream!*

Zigzagging

This is a particular sport that most capybaras adore to watch, within their own region. The contestants are capybara A-list ones; those considered to be the most famous or important.

The race begins with the word abracadabra, which activates the commencement. Capybaras gallop around a race track, at breakneck speed, making very sharp left and right turns. It is very energetic, yet highly dangerous. Sometimes, when they outmanoeuvre, or worse collide (often deliberately) with another competitor, they may get hurt. This spell will ensure that no capybara is badly injured and instead they will be peacefully subdued and feel like stopping, if they collide.

A-list event — abracadabra.
A Zigzagging extravaganza
And a real bonanza.

There'll ALWAYS be singing, dancing,
Joyful prancing.
Deadly turns via dangerous chancing.

Side-stepping skills - sequenced.
All shall be safe, cleansed,
From carelessness shown or sensed,

If present danger persists
Mind be at peace, at rest, resist.
Now sit, be still, you get the gist?

Printed in Dunstable, United Kingdom